Best Wishes
Victoria

Willie Carson

WILLIE CARSON
a Biography

Claude Duval

Willie Carson
a Biography

Stanley Paul
London Melbourne Sydney Auckland Johannesburg

Stanley Paul & Co. Ltd
An imprint of the Hutchinson Publishing Group

3 Fitzroy Square, London W1P 6JD

Hutchinson Group (Australia) Pty Ltd
30–32 Cremorne Street, Richmond South, Victoria 3121
PO Box 151, Broadway, New South Wales 2007

Hutchinson Group (NZ) Ltd
32–34 View Road, PO Box 40–086, Glenfield, Auckland 10

Hutchinson Group (SA) (Pty) Ltd
PO Box 337, Bergvlei 2012, South Africa

First published 1980
© Claude Duval 1980

Set in VIP Baskerville

Printed and bound
in Great Britain by
REDWOOD BURN LIMITED
Trowbridge & Esher

ISBN 0 09 141820 8

Contents

Acknowledgements

Tracing the remarkable career of Willie Carson has been a delightful task. So many people in racing have spoken with great warmth about the popular hero. People in his native Stirling are proud to talk of their memories of 'Billy' Carson. None more so than Mrs Thea McFarlane, who told me the story of the £4 gypsy pony which was Carson's first ride.

I was granted a helpful interview by Capt. Gerald Armstrong, Carson's first trainer. Sadly he died shortly afterwards. He died a proud man and was especially thrilled by Troy's Derby triumph.

I spent hours with Sam Armstrong, a truly remarkable trainer and personality, at his Newmarket home – previously occupied by his son-in-law Lester Piggott. Then he invited me back the next day for a second session as he had forgotten several tales about Willie!

Nick Robinson revealed the real inside story of his luckless Oaks filly Dibidale. Newmarket trainers Clive Brittain and Mick Ryan were very kind in giving up their time to talk of their association with Willie Carson.

Sir Arnold Weinstock is a very private person. He shuns publicity but was kind enough to give up some of his valuable time as head of the giant GEC business empire.

Sir Gordon Richards has always been a particular hero of mine. Typically, he was willing to grant me interviews as he spoke of Troy and his outstanding rider Willie Carson.

Thanks must also go to Central Press Photos, Gerry Cranham, Press Association, Sport and General, Sporting Pictures (UK) Ltd, the *Sun*, and their photographers Peter Jay and

Steve Markeson, and UPI for allowing the use of copyright photographs.

Lastly I must express special thanks to Lord Porchester, the Queen's racing manager, for talking to me at great length about the Royal jockey.

He told me: 'The Queen, Willie Carson and myself all have one thing in common – enthusiasm for racing.' In writing this biography to follow my books on Lester Piggott and Pat Eddery, I soon discovered that Carson – a champion like the other two – has a tremendous enthusiasm for riding winners.

In the autumn of 1979 as I sat in Lord Porchester's lounge at his magnificent Milford home, I began to wonder whether the Queen's racing manager had forgotten our appointment.

An hour late he finally came bursting through the door. Apologetically, he poured two monster-sized gin and tonics and said: 'Sorry I'm late. Troy has just this minute arrived at our Highclere stud. Isn't it exciting?'

Enthusiasm . . . and excitement! These are the passwords of the Royal racing team. My many thanks to all who have helped paint this picture in words of Willie Carson. He makes a delightful portrait.

Introduction

The fabulous field for the 200th running of the Derby in 1979 thundered round Tattenham Corner to an ear-splitting roar from thousands of race-goers.

Amid the electric atmosphere you could spot veteran Joe Mercer on Lyphard's Wish making his best way for home on the rails. Lester Piggott, the eight-times-winning Derby king, was easily recognizable in the Queen's colours on Milford.

But as a press-room colleague delicately asked: 'Where the bloody hell is Carson?' It was a fair question. He was so far back with half a mile to go that you couldn't see him from the packed grandstand.

For all the thousands who had plunged on Troy at Epsom, or were watching on television, William Fisher Hunter Carson could have been down a mine.

But at the winning line Carson came home alone. His seven-length win was the longest winning margin since 1925.

What happened in the straight to turn certain defeat into a breathtaking victory? Simple. Troy came to Epsom for the first and only time in his life . . . and was given a typical Carson ride which conquers Classics and sellers alike.

It was Carson's unique 'push, push, push' style of race-riding which urged the great Troy to go flying by his rivals. Troy made the rest look wooden horses when he got the distinct message from his coachman that he simply would not give in.

Interviewing owners and trainers about Carson is a happy task. They all have the same script-writer and say: 'Willie simply won't give in. He doesn't know when he is beaten.'

This sixty-one-inch pocket dynamo is the most loved of all

the modern-day jockeys – and that includes Lester Piggott.

The general public have a great affection for Carson. Like Sir Gordon Richards, Willie has that magical blend of integrity and genius in the saddle. It's not a commodity abundant in racing.

Even in the dingiest of back-street betting shops there's not a punter who does not cheer, 'Go on Willie,' without knowing that he has backed an out-and-out trier.

Only bad horses don't enjoy being ridden by the immensely likeable little Scotsman with the fair hair and the striking, big blue eyes.

At the end of the 1979 campaign Willie's total of winners since he started in 1962 was 1663 from 10,783 rides.

Race-goers have been marvelling at Carson for years. But I pick out one race in which, if I had not seen it with my own eyes, I would never have believed what happened.

It wasn't a Classic or valuable handicap. Just a one-mile race for three-year-old fillies at Doncaster in September 1978. To me it summed up the brilliance of the flying Scot.

Miss Noname was the filly – bred ironically by High Top, who was Carson's first Classic winner. She was owned by Stanley Powell, a great enthusiast who lost a few friends when he begged them not to back his first-ever runner, The Industan at Epsom, shortly before he flew in at 100–6.

His horses are usually named after a combination of the partners in the purchase, hence The Brianstan and The Stuartstan. Le Johnson was so named because the Jockey Club thought Powell had too many 'The's'!

Miss Noname had seven names rejected and in desperation Powell settled for an obvious last resort. I watched the Doncaster race with the owner.

At half-way Powell's face was a sad sight. He certainly didn't enjoy what he was watching through his binoculars.

Four furlongs from home Miss Noname was quickly being renamed again. But Carson thought differently. He put his head down and started to ride for his life.

Recalls Powell: 'Two furlongs out Willie was stone last. We had no chance. I put my bins down and lost interest.

'Then suddenly, like a man inspired, Willie started to get

Miss Noname into top gear and they started to fly. They went by one horse after another. It was incredible. I couldn't believe the ground that Willie made up and eventually he pounced on the unlucky runner-up to win by a neck.

'It nearly gave me a heart attack. It was sheer brilliance.'

I fully concur. I've never forgotten the power-packed finish that Carson rode that day. I've seen these finishes before and since but that one sticks in my admiring mind.

John Sutcliffe, trainer of Miss Noname, said: 'No other jockey on earth would have won on that horse.' What further praise is needed?

Powell was a war hero and made seven daring escapes. His mother received the dubious telegram half-way through the war: 'We are pleased to tell you that your son has been captured by the Germans.'

He even faced a firing squad and walked away. It was a plot to break down the prisoners for information. Now he jokes: 'That was nearly as bad as getting a horse beaten by a short head.'

Powell is one of hundreds of owners who rave about Carson. He says: 'He's a great little fella. He begged me to keep The Adrianstan in training. He promised me that he was good enough to win a big handicap. Sure enough, The Adrianstan won the Victoria Cup. But for Willie he would have been sent to the sales.'

Sir Gordon Richards, a great Carson admirer, jokes: 'I am exactly 4 feet 11½ inches tall. I'm hoping that I live long enough to reach 5 feet.'

Willie, the kid from the Stirling prefab who was to become the Queen's jockey, has already pipped the 5-foot mark – and has an inch to spare. It's often that same little margin which gives a Carson-partnered horse the advantage in a photograph.

Critics may claim that he has only one basic style of riding. There may be an element of truth in that. But, my word, how effective his tactics have been in recent years.

And when race fans discuss the great jockeys of this century Willie Carson can walk tall alongside the best of them.

You will read of the warmth of people in racing towards

Carson. Lords of the realm love him for driving their horses into the winner's enclosures. The Queen is a great fan.

But bookies curse him when they have to dig deep into their satchels after a Miss Noname-type display.

Trainer Mick Ryan sums him up well. He says: 'Willie always wins on horses that he should win on . . . and on quite a few he has no right to win on.

'That's the hallmark of a genius.'

There's never a dull moment when Willie is around. It's doubtful if there has ever been a more popular guest on the BBC's *A Question of Sport*. In the autumn of 1979 when it came to his two specialist subjects he was at his cheeky best.

Asked David Coleman: 'Who was the last Irishman to win the Irish Derby?'

After pondering Willie answered: 'Pat Glennon.'

'Wrong' said Coleman – 'It's Pat Eddery.'

'But he's lived over here for years,' ventured Carson, amid hoots of laughter from the audience.

Coleman then asked: 'Which was the last filly to win the King George?'

Replied Willie: 'Dahlia.'

'Wrong,' said Coleman again. 'Pawnesse is the answer.'

'But Dahlia won it twice,' was Willie's quick reply. Again he had the audience in stitches.

He may not know all the answers . . . but when he's in the saddle, Willie Carson is never slow to gallop himself into the winner's enclosure.

Nobody questions his genius.

1 'I thought the other boys would kill him'

The rise of Willie Carson to be first jockey to the Queen is a fairy-tale – pure and simple.

It's the kind of nags-to-riches story which not even a dreamy-eyed Hollywood script-writer could ever pen.

And amazingly it was a sixpenny seat in a Stirling cinema which started the Carson fairy-tale – the remarkable background of the wee Scots kid who was to gallop into the record books of the Turf and every punter's heart.

He was born in Stirling, the Gateway to the Highlands, on 16 November 1942. This makes him a Scorpio and he certainly falls into the type: 'Scorpios move and speak quickly. They have an open, friendly manner. They can destroy their bodies with excesses, melancholy or hard work but can also build them back at will from a critical illness.'

He certainly has proved the latter on several occasions.

He was christened William Fisher Hunter Carson after a great uncle, who was a missionary to America. His parents now live in Newmarket where Carson has bought them a house.

His father, Tommy, was a warehouse foreman for a banana firm. His mother, May, who is only 4 feet 9 inches tall, has played a vital role in the formation of the Royal jockey's personality.

When he was twelve he returned home from a matinee showing of the film *Rainbow Jacket* and said: 'I'm going to be a jockey.' His parents were surprised. As he was good with his hands they had hoped that he might become a joiner.

Willie in fact told a careers officer at his school that he

wanted to become a jockey. But the careers officer told him: 'You'll never make a jockey. Racing is not for you. You'll become far too heavy and have weight problems.'

But Willie would not be persuaded that racing was not for him . . . and this was when a very special woman came into his life: Mrs Thea McFarlane, owner of the local riding school.

She told me at her fifty-four-horse Scottish Equitation Centre, now switched to Dunblane: 'Billy's mother approached me and asked whether I would take the youngster for a few riding lessons.'

Mrs McFarlane, who always refers to her star ex-pupil as Billy, went on: 'His mother used to work in a restaurant that I used to use. Quite frankly I think she sent him to me to keep him quiet.

'He had nagged her rotten about being a jockey and his mother thought that he would work it out of his system if he had a few lessons. They never dreamt that he would actually make a go of the horse-riding.

'I can remember the first time he came for lessons. He was so tiny I couldn't believe. He was minute but had enormous blue eyes. Maybe he was a little shy because he was always silent. There was almost a strange sort of quietness about him. He was in no way the same outgoing character which he is today.

'I know that his mother thought that he'd just have a lesson and become disenchanted with the whole idea of being a jockey. I think that he was only about 4 feet 6 inches when he first came to me. That's the outstanding memory of him – he was very, very small.

'At first I must admit that I never thought that he would make it as a rider, perhaps we always think that. So many kids want to become show-jumpers and yet so few actually make it.

'I thought that he was too small and frail to be a jockey. I didn't think that he would be strong enough to stand up to stable life.

'When he went into stables I was frightened that as he was so small the other boys would kill him.'

The Carson fairy-tale now takes in the world of gypsies. Recalls Mrs McFarlane: 'I was walking with my father round the Duke of Portland's estate one day and spotted a lovely little pony with a caravan of the romanies.

'My father went over and asked whether he could buy the pony, who had been bought up by the romanies from Dartmoor. The man said he would sell for only £4 as the pony was a squealer and would never be any good for riding or driving.

'Actually the old romany was wrong. She did squeal a bit when you ran your hand down one of her legs. But we had a vet to her, broke her in and she was a perfect pony for children to learn on.

'When Billy walked into the riding school I knew that the pony, who was called Jill, was just ideal for him. The little chestnut mare was 11 hands.

'They got on well. Billy hardly ever said a word and I used to have to shout and yell at him to get him to learn to ride. Of course, he fell off several times, Jill used to take off and go a fair old pace.

'But he never cried. He got straight back up again every time.

'I tried to teach him the basic classic seat. I didn't pull up his stirrups and try to teach him the sort of style he would have to adopt if he did go ahead and join a stable.

'I never tried to teach him anything which wasn't quite in my range at a riding school. Perhaps I did give him a chance. One thing I did try and impress on him was to scrub Jill along. I used to tell him that he should give her an extra inch or two of rein if he thought it right.

'I charged Billy ten shillings an hour for his weekly lesson and he used to do a newspaper round to pay for the lesson. He has wonderful parents and he was always very smartly dressed.

'But being so small he used to get bullied a little by the other boys. He used to dislike being seen wearing jodhpurs on the nine-mile-round bike ride to the lessons. He used to bring the jodhpurs in a little paper bag and then change when he got to the riding school.

'I told him not to be so soft. But it was difficult. You'd never believe just how frail and tiny he was.

'Jill died in my arms. She was forty years old and was a great family pet. It was a lucky day for us and Billy when we met those romanies. I then switched Billy to another pony called

Wings. When I took part in the *This Is Your Life* programme on Billy they wanted me to bring the small grey mare down to London but she was too old to travel so they came up and filmed her here. Sadly, she's dead now too.'

Willie's newspaper-round exploits are still recalled by Jim Hogg, a former City Councillor, who owned a newsagent's shop in Cowane Street, Stirling.

He said: 'He may be the greatest jockey in the world but when I knew him he had another title . . . the smallest news-paper boy in the world.

'When he first came to me I never thought that he would be big enough to carry all the newspapers. I'd never seen anything so small. Perhaps all the walking and pedalling around the town helped to strengthen his legs up a bit.

'Most lads get fed up with the early-morning starts and chuck it in after two weeks. Billy stayed on for two years.'

Being so small it was obvious that Carson would get some stick from his class-mates. Recalls Mrs McFarlane: 'I know that after a while his father bought Billy some boxing gloves and gave him a lesson for an hour.

'Then he opened the front door and sent him out in the street. From then on he was handing out a few hidings rather than being on the receiving end the whole time.

'After a while it was obvious that Billy would go into a racing stable. I wrote to two trainers and then somebody told me that Captain Gerald Armstrong was a kind old man and would be ideal for Billy. Anyway his mother did not want him to go too far south, and Middleham wasn't a million miles away.

'After Billy had been there a week I got a phone call from Captain Armstrong. He said, "Have you got any more Billy Carsons?" He was delighted that the lad knew all about muck-ing out the stables and was keen to learn.'

Mrs McFarlane reveals that if it had not been for May Carson the great fairy-tale would not have come under start-er's orders.

She told me: 'Middleham is a pretty bleak sort of place and Billy went down there in the middle of the winter. It's not much fun for lads and Billy was desperately homesick for Stirling.

'He wrote to his mother several times during the first year at

Middleham begging her to let him come home. He even wrote to me and asked me to try and persuade his mother to allow him to get out of racing.

'But his mother was determined. She said that he had taken the trouble to have lessons and they had spent a lot of money getting him clothes to go to Middleham.

'Added to this, his mother pointed out that he had signed his apprenticeship and there was no way that she would allow him to break his contract.

'It's a fact that Billy would probably have been working in a cigarette factory or some other job in Stirling but for the fact that his mother refused to let him come home.

'It's always tricky when boys are pitched straight into stables. But after a while Billy started to enjoy the life.'

When wee Willie was eight he had joined the Lifeboys. But his head was so tiny that he could not find a cap small enough to fit him. In the end he had to wear one stuffed with paper.

He only wore it twice before it was stolen. As a small boy he was always finding other lads taking liberties. He didn't go to another meeting of the Lifeboys and told his father, 'If they can do that to me, they can do anything.'

Willie weighed in at six pounds when he was born, which is exactly three times Yves Saint-Martin's initial weigh-in. Not unnaturally he was known as 'Titch' as a youngster. The film *Rainbow Jacket*, which was about a boy who rose to jockey stardom, sparked his interest in racing.

Until then he had only watched his father when he made his selections for his weekly one-shilling wager. There were no racecourses nearby and until he went to Middleham he had not actually seen racehorses in action.

Locals in Stirling still recall 'Billy Carson' with pride. On the sporting front the same town also produced Billy Bremner, the flame-haired wing-half who found fame with Leeds United in their heyday.

Many still remember seeing little Carson struggling under the weight of his newspaper load over the old Customs Bridge which spans the River Forth at the eastern foot of Stirling Castle.

As Brough Scott wrote: 'Early workers who noticed the tiny

biking figure half-hidden by the delivery bag and muttered, "Yon laddie will go far," didn't know how prophetic they were being.'

Brough recalls one interview with Carson at Doncaster. They were in full flow when a Doncaster official decided that the presentation of some prizes should take place bang in front of Brough and his subject. Viewers heard Willie quickly sum up the dilemma. 'Now we're stuffed,' he observed.

After his Derby triumph on Troy a joyous Willie was interviewed by Julian Wilson for BBC TV. The impish little rider grabbed Wilson's top hat and wore it during the interview. At one stage he tugged it down over his ears and looked the original Mad Hatter. Happy moments which he is unlikely to forget.

Beaming, he admitted: 'Yes, I may go out and have half a gin and tonic tonight.'

As owners point out regularly, there may be a happy-go-lucky side to Carson. But beneath the infectious laughter and broad grin ticks a serious brain.

He knows that in some ways he has had to pay a big price for the stardom and wealth which he now enjoys. To be in the chase for the champion jockeys' title you must virtually say good-bye to your summer. Days off are as rare as double rainbows. With air travel so easy two meetings a day are a doddle and then there is always the lure of big French prize money on Sundays.

After his first championship our weary hero slept for five days. To keep up his relentless search for winners puts one under tremendous strains.

Sadly, Willie's marriage did not last under the pressures of his hard-earned stardom. In January 1974 the Fleet Street gossip columnists were on the warpath – never a pleasant experience for anybody.

Willie cut short a trip to Hong Kong to dash home to his wife Carole when reports first linked him with the successful lady jockey Suzanne Kane, daughter of a wealthy company director. 'It's all newspaper talk,' claimed Willie.

But sadly to many people in racing, the storm clouds which had gathered were not an illusion. And Willie was soon at Suzanne's bed-side in Oxford's Radcliffe Royal Infirmary where she recovered from severe head injuries sustained while out hunting.

By mid-March Willie was living with trainer Clive Brittain and his wife, just 200 yards from his family home. By 1977 divorce was a reality, and in November he was officially divorced from his childhood sweetheart. They had been married for fourteen years.

Willie now lives near Dick Hern's Berkshire stables. Devoted Suzanne Kane is rarely not at the races when Willie produces his superb efforts.

Carole played a big part in Willie's early success. She booked many of his rides and spent hours on the telephone arranging his weekly schedule. Now the man behind the scenes is Willie's hard-working secretary, Ted Eley, who masterminds much of his organization from Newmarket.

He spends hours on the telephone arranging spare rides for Willie when he is not required by Dick Hern. Admits Ted: 'The little fella is stronger and better than ever. He has the stamina of ten men. His appetite for winners is as keen as ever after twenty years. And he'll go anywhere to ride a winner.'

Ted Eley spends hours going through the form book to make sure that Willie picks the right horse when he has the choice of mounts in a race. Relates Ted, a back-room boy who never goes racing: 'In 1977 we were offered five rides in the Royal Hunt Cup. I watched on television and sweated a bit till he came storming through in the final furlong on My Hussar. Thankfully he had picked the right one.'

Mrs Thea McFarlane, who had such an important influence at the vital formative stage of Willie's riding career, may now be extending her help to the family.

The Carsons had three sons and Neil, who is the split image of his father, went to the riding school of Mrs McFarlane when on holiday in Perthshire. Neil is an all-round athlete, a 100-metres runner for Suffolk and a useful centre-forward. But he fancies a career in racing and was involved at Clive Brittain's stables.

Tony faced fears of being too heavy for the Flat but was a useful member of Michael Stoute's team at Newmarket. Ross, the youngster of the trio, suffers badly from hay fever and did not enjoy visits to racing stables. He is the academic of the family and is more interested in books than bridles.

So Thea McFarlane could be involved in producing another Carson champion.

Yet to think that she started Willie on the path to fame with an ex-crippled little chestnut mare called Jill. She cost a mere £4, and when Willie went to Middleham, Thea McFarlane thought that Willie was so frail that 'the other boys would kill him'.

Twenty years later Willie powered to victory in the Derby on Troy, valued at £7.5 million. Times have certainly changed for the world's smallest newspaper boy.

Now he's making the headlines . . . not struggling across Stirling Bridge with the delivery bag.

2 'Thank you for putting me on the right path'

Pride goes before a fall. But in Captain Gerald Armstrong's life his proudest moment came long after a horror fall. The distinguished amateur rider turned trainer was the first man in racing to fashion the future career of Willie Carson.

Shortly after Troy's unforgettable Epsom Derby triumph the postman at Middleham had a long trudge up the drive of the Tupgill stables.

When Gerald Armstrong, elder brother of Sam Armstrong, opened the letter he found a splendid colour photograph of Troy. On the back was a simple message: 'Many thanks for your congratulations. Troy's win gave me a great thrill. Thank you for putting me on the right path. Hope you are in good health. Regards, Willie.'

Carson did not let Troy's Derby win go by without remembering the veteran figure up in the Yorkshire Dales who 'put him on the right path'.

For as Gerald Armstrong told me proudly: 'I tell people that I never trained a Derby winner. But at least I was a man responsible for a Derby-winning jockey.'

Sadly, just a few months after Troy's triumph Gerald Armstrong died at the age of eighty.

It was in the Yorkshire town of Middleham that Carson had his first job in racing. On the bleak Middleham Moor he had his introduction to racehorses.

Middleham's castle ruins date back to the twelfth century. The stone walls of the surrounding fields make this isolated spot a suitable location for Emmerdale Farm. Tiny cafés called The Nosebag and The Stable Door Teashop overlook the cobbled town square with its ancient monument.

Middleham Moor has become a popular training centre and the town can boast Neville Crump, 'Squeak' Fairhurst, Chris Thornton, Dick Peacock, Steve Nesbitt, Jumbo Wilkinson and colourful Harry Blackshaw amongst its trainers today.

Gerald Armstrong had retired as a trainer, but he recalled with pride the day Carson entered racing. The picture of Troy had pride of place on his mantlepiece when Gerald told me: 'We Armstrongs have always had a lot of apprentice boys in our stables.

'My father Robert Ward Armstrong was one of the last men the Jockey Club allowed to train and ride at the same time. We are a Cumberland family and he was only sixteen when he started training in our home town of Penrith.

'In 1923 father moved from Penrith to Tupgill in Middleham. His main patron was Lord Lonsdale. Perhaps his best success came in 1888 when he trained Dan Dancer to win the Ascot Stakes. Conditions at Ascot were so primitive in those days that Dan Dancer had to spend the night before the race in a cow byre.'

Gerald, like his brother Sam, had a thousand racing memories. But when he talked of Carson he recalled the past with great affection.

'I had placed an advertisement in a paper for apprentices,' said Gerald. 'But at about that time I was approached by Carson's parents from Stirling. They said that he had been to a riding school run by some woman. Like my father I always had a few boys in the stables. I never took them in pig-iron state. Ideally, I wanted a lad who had ridden a little bit.

'I remembered the day well when Carson's parents came to my house with little Willie. He was a titch, no taller than a chair. Some trainers today show the intelligence of rabbits and take on 6-foot boys weighing 12 stone. They are mad to take on these navvies.

'The secret of having good apprentices is to take on boys of not more than 5 feet 7 inches and not more than fourteen years old. They must start light.

'My father always made them start light. He was great with apprentices and turned Harry Carr into the King's jockey.

Harry's father was my father's travelling head lad for many years.

'My father turned Carr into a King's jockey. I suppose I could claim to have turned Carson into a Queen's jockey.

'Of course, he was terribly nervous when he first came to me with his parents. He hadn't been outside his home town of Stirling before. I went out to a field and put Carson up on a Shetland pony.

'I told him to trot round the field on the pony and then to have a little canter. I was pleased with the way he shaped and could tell that the woman who had taught him had done a good job. Little Willie was always very keen to become a jockey and we signed him up to be indentured to me there and then.

'I can't claim to be the first person to put him on a horse. He had a little experience of horses – not racehorses. He was no stylist but after he cantered round the field I had no hesitation in saying, "I'll take the boy."

'He slept in the dormitory with all the other boys. I was in the 5th Lancers in the army and ran my stables very much on army lines. I was very keen on discipline. My records show that the first week's wages for Carson came to two-and-six.

'It was a hard introduction to racing. No thrills. Some trainers idolize their apprentices and drive them to the races in their cars like royalty. Mine travelled rough with the horses.

'I kept him in his place. He probably didn't thank me at the time but he had a good schooling in the art of race-riding.

'He was the best-mannered boy I ever had. He went to the top because he was the most successful. He always conducted himself well and his integrity was always beyond question.'

Gerald rode over a hundred winners as an amateur rider and trained hundreds of winners. His proudest moment came in 1934 when he rode Whitehead to win at Ripon in the colours of the King. The best horse he trained was probably Thankerton.

His whole life changed after one horror fall at the old Lewes racecourse. He recounts: 'I was riding a horse called The Sponger. As we turned into the straight two or three horses fell, and as I lay moaning on the ground a horse kicked me in the head. It was a bad injury but I did ride again after the fall.

'It's funny how Carson ended up at Stanley House as first

jockey to Lord Derby because I spent many years there as assistant to the Hon. George Lambton and a nicer man I never met.

'Many people liken Tommy Weston, Lord Derby's jockey in those days, to Willie Carson. All I would say is that Willie was a more polite type of character with owners.

'I do claim a little bit of the credit for Carson. I gave him his chance and he took it with both hands. From that first canter round the field he was always mustard-keen to learn.

'In those early days I insisted that they did not use a whip. My boys had to have several rides before I would allow them to have the use of a whip. I was only a small trainer and never had any expensive horses. I simply couldn't afford to lose my horses and I used to tell my boys, "Don't knock this horse about. I don't want him upset or abused."'

When Gerald decided to retire from training in 1962 he realized that he had an outstanding riding prospect in Carson. He said: 'I got straight on the telephone to my brother Fred [he never called him Sam] and he agreed to take him.'

Said Gerald: 'Like me he always had a few good boys in his yard. He had seen Carson a few times and liked his style. We soon agreed to have Carson's indentures transferred. It was on Saturday evenings, after dinner, that Carson probably got his best teaching.

'Like my father I used to have Saturday evening instruction sessions. All the lads would meet in the mess-room and I would go to a lot of trouble teaching them.

'I used to stress to them the correct way to shorten the reins. I would sit on an old form with a saddle strapped round it and demonstrate the proper way to shorten the reins and then change the whip from the left hand to the right hand.

'It makes me wince when I see some of the cowboys on television today trying to change their whip hands. Pretty well all the accidents we have in racing would be prevented if boys had been taught properly how to shorten the reins.

'Carson had a tough upbringing. There were no thrills at Middleham. It was hard graft, army discipline, and precious little financial reward at the end of the week.

'Of course, a lot of boys hated it and couldn't get out of

racing quick enough. But Willie was always keen to learn. I was a very proud man when I was invited down to London to take part in the *This Is Your Life* programme when Willie was the subject.'

In 1962 – Willie's first year as an apprentice rider – the tiny Scot had twenty-six rides. He was unplaced twenty-one times but had three thirds, a second . . . and his first winner.

In Middleham the cheerful little apprentice was always known as 'Scottie' Carson. His first taste of the winner's enclosure came at nearby Catterick on 19 July 1962 in the Apprentices Handicap. Riding 6–1 shot Pinkers Pond, he made all the running in the seven-furlong race to win by an easy six lengths. I wonder how many hundreds of times since this moderate little Catterick race Carson has powered horses home in photo-finishes. But his first win was an easy one. Significantly the other apprentices in the race never went on to achieve the fame and fortune which lay ahead for Carson. The other riders were Plan, Dodd, Hill, Butler, Youds and Crossley. On the same day at Catterick the then cock of the north, Edward Hide, rode a four-timer on Nickican, Dynabella, Partita, and Val Bug.

Pinkers Pond was owned by Manchester textile manufacturer Sidney Bernstein. A Welsh Jew by birth, Bernstein loved a bet. Under the name of Mr Sid Scott he used to race greyhounds at Salford and, if they were good enough, at Belle Vue, Manchester.

A bachelor, Bernstein set off one day for Wolverhampton races where he had runners. On his way he was involved in a near-car-crash on a bit of dual-carriageway. Luckily he came to rest just a few inches from a tree and his car was not damaged. Rather shaken he turned back and did not go on to the races. Sadly, within ten days he died. The shock of the near-accident obviously had a delayed affect.

It was the Armstrong brothers, Gerald and Fred, who put Carson 'on the right path'. It was a tough, relentless road. Hard work was the order of the day, but it made him the outstanding jockey he is today.

I like the advice Robert Armstrong senior – father of Gerald and Fred – gave his two boys on his death bed.

He told them: 'In life with people always keep the best possible company for yourself. In racing always keep the worst possible company for your horses.'

3 The Armstrong Academy

Willie Carson has been associated with the vast equine armies of Bernard van Cutsem, Clive Brittain, Barry Hills and Dick Hern over the years, but the man who really fashioned his career was the astute Newmarket trainer Sam Armstrong. Yet he started in a Middleham yard in Yorkshire with just one horse.

Sam, the younger brother to Carson's first master Gerald Armstrong, held a trainer's licence from 1924 to 1972. Besides being one of the most shrewd trainers, he developed a wonderful reputation for tutoring apprentices. Besides Carson, future jumping champion Josh Gifford, Wally Swinburn, Paul Tulk, Jack Egan, Kipper Lynch, David East, Willie Snaith and the late Michael Hayes were a few of the star pupils to go through his riding academy.

When Gerald Armstrong retired at the end of the 1962 Flat season Carson's indentures at Middleham were switched to brother Sam at Newmarket. The wee Scot could not have gone to a better – or harder – school.

Recalls Willie: 'In October that year I moved down to Newmarket. At first I thought that I was on loan but then I realized that my old guv'nor had decided to retire.

'When I first heard that I was going to Mr Armstrong I was scared stiff. I knew that he had the reputation of being the hardest man in racing. But he was a super trainer and he taught me a hell of a lot.'

Kipper Lynch is still an ardent admirer of his initial tutor. He says: 'You can tell an ex-Armstrong apprentice anywhere. There's no mistaking them . . . they're always the best turned-out. Trim and proper.'

Sam handed over his Saint Gatien yard to son Robert in 1972. His daughter Susan married Lester Piggott, and her support and keen business brain has played a vital role in the making of the maestro.

In 1962 when Carson first moved to Newmarket he was one of racing's starry-eyed lads, dreaming of riding winners and making the grade as a jockey.

By the spring of 1979 and the Craven meeting he returned to headquarters as the champion jockey. And no man gets more satisfaction from his success than Sam Armstrong.

He and his wife now live in the tree-lined Avenue in Newmarket in Lester Piggott's former home, then called Florizel after the horse Susan rode to win the Newmarket Town Plate.

The timbered house bang opposite the world-famous Tattersalls sales ring has been renamed Ashgill, after the Middleham yard where life as an English trainer started for Armstrong.

'Ah, my boys,' says Armstrong proudly, like a retired headmaster. But that is what Sam, who was born in 1904, was – an unsurpassed teacher, and Carson was lucky to join his class.

Sam coached his lads in the old way. It was hard but it made so many of the jockeys the success they are today.

In the lounge of the house where Lester returned after so many of his triumphs all over the world, Sam recalls with pride: 'The Queen was out in India a few years ago and went racing in Calcutta. It was for the Queen's Plate and Swinburn won the race. She told him, "It's nice to see six Armstrong boys in the same race."

'It was a fact too – Swinburn, Carson, Lynch, Tulk, East and Charlie Garton. I always had a rule that I never took any boy who had been with any other trainer before. I never took them. I always wanted to make them into jockeys for myself.

'Willie Carson was an exception in two ways. He had been elsewhere before and he was the only boy who ever signed indentures with me who got married before he was twenty-one.

'I was happy to make an exception taking him from elsewhere as my brother Gerald said that he was definitely of above-average ability and it would be a shame if he went out of racing.

'From those very early days he was always a good boy. He certainly was always bright. He was always anxious to get on. Often in the winter I'd send my boys off to India and they learnt quite a bit out there.

'Carson always took advantage of anything that he was taught. He was always keen to watch the more senior jockeys' riding work in the mornings. He would have ridden early-morning gallops with Lester in those days.

'He never had any weight problems and was always a handy weight. He was very strong for his weight.

'Over the years I have seen all the top riders – I had a licence for fifty years and several of the old-timers used to ride for me when I started. Willie reminds me very much of Tommy Weston – strength is their greatest asset. Old Tommy served his time in Middleham as well.

'He was a grand chap. He rode a horse for me at Redcar one day and I fancied it a little. We had a little investment but he finished second. I'll always remember Weston telling me, "If I had given him one, he'd have won." I told him, "I wish the Lord you had."

'In my time I would have to pick out four jockeys as the best I have witnessed. I've got to put Lester first and not for family reasons. He's got a wonderful brain. He never stops thinking during a race, always knows what he intends to do next. The hours he must have spent studying the form-book over the years must be amazing.

'Gordon Richards was marvellous, of course. Just look at his record. Steve Donoghue was a pretty rider – nice, quiet style.

'And in my top four I would put Willie Carson. At his weight I can safely say that I've never seen a better jockey. At around the 7 stone 10 pounds mark I would say he's the best. I put him just in front of Tommy Weston.

'Carson was entitled to be champion. Hard work and bags of determination got the rewards they deserved.

'Like Gordon he battles on, simply won't give in and he's a very effective rider. They are very similar – perpetual motion.

'Another of my little tricks was always to tell an apprentice to style himself on somebody. I used to find a man of similar build and tell the boy that so-and-so was no better man to copy. Gordon was two or three pounds heavier but I told Carson to model himself on him. A lad of Josh Gifford's build and I told him to try and copy Lester.

'I always liked Carson as a character. We got on well and when he was out of his time he signed on for another year.

'The secret of my success with boys can be summed up in one word . . . discipline. I sometimes had to be hard to discipline boys to do things in the proper way. They always wore caps when riding work, and I insisted that they wore a hat whenever they were parading a horse around before a race on the race-course.

'Carson like all my lads was not allowed to use a whip until he had ridden five winners. My father was always very strict on that as well. I used to encourage them to use their hands rather than their whips. After I had taught them to use their hands I would allow them to carry a short whip and then in time the big ones.

'Carson was never one to come back after a race with excuses. Some lads would always come back with the same old story, "Sorry, guv'nor, was interferred with." The next week I'd get the same tale. I told one boy, "It's about time I heard others tell me that you knocked them over." With Carson there were never excuses. He soon got to know how to race-ride.

'When boys had outside rides I always used to make them report to me in the evening and tell me how they had got on. Charlie Garton came back one night and I called him in. "How did you get on?" I asked. "Was the owner pleased?" Charlie replied, "Oh yes, Sir, very delighted." I said, "Where did you finish?" and he admitted, "Last." I told him, "Yes, I bet the owner must have been very delighted."

'Most Sundays I would contact Norman Fairchild of the Press Association, who dealt with the jockeys. He would tell me if certain horses did not have jockeys for the following day and I would get straight on the phone and organize rides for my boys.'

Race-cards always used to print the trainer as F. L. Armstrong and looking back with a smile he recounts, 'Sam is a nickname – had it for years. My older brother and sister used to look at me when I was a baby and remark how dark my hair was. I was called a Little Black Sambo and I've been known as Sam ever since. Often, even today, I have to think twice when I get to the bottom of a letter to know how actually to sign my name.

'I hate nicknames. I made sure that my two children, Robert and Susan, were never called anything else.

'Kipper Lynch got his nickname because he was so small. His father was a fish merchant in the Old Kent Road and he'd never even sat on a horse until he walked into my yard. I don't think he'd even seen a horse before. I remember Susan calling me to the window to look out when he first got on a horse in the paddock. We all expected him to fall over but he was another natural rider. He was tiny.

'Wally Swinburn came from Birkenhead and weighed 4 stone when he first joined me. Willie Snaith weighed just 3 stone 6 pounds but he gained his first win in 1946 on Newmarket's July course when he beat Gordon Richards by a head on Chotta Shaib.

'I used to give the lads their pocket money twice a week. I worked it out that if they had the lot on a Friday they would probably blow it all by the Sunday so it was best in two parts.

'In those days the boys were indentured for seven years. At the end of it all they used to get a nice little sum. For inside rides the trainer would get the earnings, and half the outside rides.'

Ironically Sam, the man whose strictness probably created Carson's will to win, only had one ride on the Flat himself . . . when he was beaten by a neck.

He had two years training in Ireland before he moved to Ashgill, Middleham. He well remembers his first horse . . . and the only one in his yard at the time!

'I played rugby for Carlisle, trained near there and saddled my first winner there,' he says. 'But I was at Pontefract one day and bought a horse called William's Mount out of a seller for £270.

'The Newmarket trainer, Herbert Toon, who I bought the horse from, thought that I was crazy. He told me, "He hasn't eaten a thing since he left Newmarket. You've bought nothing but trouble." He laughed at me.

'But I got him home and fed him up well. I put his manger on the floor and the plan worked. Horses are naturally used to eating off the ground. He went on to win several races for me.'

It was mid-way through the Second World War that Armstrong was approached to buy yearlings for the Maharajah of Baroda, who he had never even met. 'Among those I bought were the sprinter Rah Quma Kumar, Akkarje and The Yuvaraj, who won all his five races as a two-year-old in 1945. Those three won twelve in all,' says Sam.

'Eventually the Maharajah persuaded me to come south and I bought Warren Place for £53,000. Later I moved to the Saint Gatien yard,' says Sam, whose weather-beaten face can't conceal thousands of early-morning gallop sessions on Newmarket Heath. But he has bravely conquered two heart attacks, and on both occasions came out of hospital much quicker than doctors forecast.

'Moving my team from Middleham to Newmarket just after the war was a major operation. We hired a special train from Leyland to Newmarket and moved fifty-five horses, the staff, beds, canteen, etc. – they all went on the train. I boxed up every horse myself and saw them off at the other end – all without a scratch.

'In 1945 I paid a record 28,000 guineas for Sayajirao for the Maharajah. Actually I had two other owners – John Hamer and Captain Tremain – who were after him. I only made the one bid on behalf of the Maharajah and the other two were very annoyed with me afterwards.

'In 1947 we had a terrible pre-season spell of weather. From December to March we were simply snowed under, and I couldn't get Sayajirao as ready as I would have liked.

'He was a gross horse and needed plenty of work. Here was a record-priced yearling – and the record lasted for a long time – and I couldn't work him at all. At one stage the weather was so bad with big snow drifts that we were completely marooned at Warren Place for three days. Finally we were able to get a wagon through via Moulton and the Bury Road to get provisions. We were getting mighty low on food for the lads.

'He won the Lingfield Derby Trial, the Irish Derby and the St Leger. He was third in the English Guineas and the Derby. He was very unlucky – I was never able to get him quite right.

Top left: Willie Carson was 6 pounds at his first weigh-in . . . and even as an infant had a good seat

Right: As a kid Willie hated to be seen in jodhpurs. But here he poses in his parents' garden

Below left: The same fair hair and big blue eyes – Willie as a Sam Armstrong apprentice

Classic glory . . . Willie's first Classic win after making every yard on High Top in the 1972 2000 Guineas. Runner-up was subsequent Derby winner Roberto, ridden by Bill Williamson

A friendly pat in the rain for High Top, van Cutsem had told Willie, 'See how fast you can gallop,' and High Top was never headed

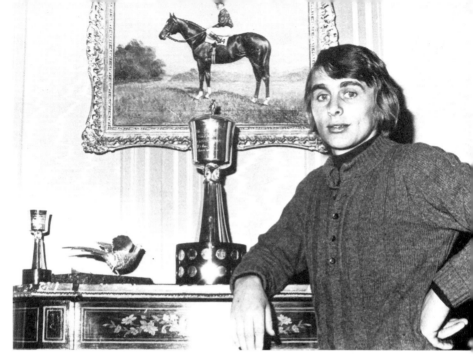

Willie is seen with the Champion Jockey trophy he won in 1973. In the background is his prized portrait of High Top

Willie explains a point to the late Bernard van Cutsem. The trainer used to say before races, '. . . I've had a few bob on here, Willie.' Sometimes it was thousands

Sir Gordon Richards – 'Willie has a style all of his own,' says the fabulous rider of 4870 winners

Major Dick Hern – 'Willie simply never gives in. He doesn't know when he is beaten,' says the trainer of Troy

Lord Derby – 'You always have a good laugh with Willie,' says the man who gave Carson his biggest break

Sam Armstrong – 'At his weight I've never seen a better jockey than Willie Carson,' says the former Newmarket trainer

But it would have meant working him with snow up to his belly and that would have been madness.'

Armstrong trained over 1350 winners on the Flat. A fine record as there was far less racing in those days. He always tried to get his horses to fitness and then try and run up a sequence of victories.

He says: 'Training horses is like farming. You have crops in spring, summer and autumn. When the horses have bloomed you get on and go harvesting.

'Had I trained Sayajirao in the north I might have been able to get him fitter. In bad times up there I used to go to the sands at Whitby after stabling the horses in lock-up garages.'

Early days in Newmarket were not all easy for Armstrong, although he does recall first seeing his future son-in-law Lester when he was two months old and in his cot at Keith Piggott's Wantage stables.

'In those days you virtually had to produce your birth certificate before the Jockey Club would give you a licence to train in Newmarket. They laid down conditions for me but I said that if I came it would be without any conditions.

'The Jockey Club could even decide which owners you could train horses for. The late William Hill wanted horses with me, but they would not allow it as he was a bookmaker and they were determined that no bookmaker should have a horse trained in the town.

'I trained for virtually every nationality under the sun – funny though, I don't think I ever had a Spaniard.

'Indians, Chinese, Australians, Brazilians, Greeks, Irish, French, Italians, Germans, Swiss, Egyptians . . . I had them all.

'The Maharani of Baroda took her horses away from me three times . . . and brought them back three times. They were great believers in horoscopes and crystal balls etc.

'I trained six winners at one Epsom Derby meeting but her horse-boxes came to take the horses away. The horoscope must have said that they'd have better luck with a fair-haired man.

'Another time I was in Paris to run Royal Empire in a big race and I had a message to ring the Baroda. He said that all the horses were to leave me the next day. I'd trained nothing but winners for him for a week. ·

'Funny people those Orientals – but we had good times mainly. They always came back. I never made the mistake of begging to keep the horses. I never wanted to be under any obligation.

'The late Major Holliday got rid of his trainer and I got a friend to introduce me. He told me that he wanted me to buy two yearlings but stressed: "If they are no good I want you to tell me." By May I could tell that they were not any good at all and told him so. He took the horses away to Ireland and he never sent me another horse.

'Twenty years later at Chester I was working my horses early one morning when my ex-travelling head lad Walter Gill pointed to a horse and said, "That's the horse Tommy Gosling got the sack over." I said, "Why?" Said Walter, "Because he told Major Holliday that the horse was no good and that's the only thing he hated." It took me twenty years to find out that he didn't want to hear if they were useless at all.

'I learnt from my father that you had to go out and get owners. Ravi Tikkoo had Steel Pulse with me and he'd done well in his two-year-old career, just getting beaten in France and in the Observer Gold Cup.

'One night I was driving home from London and passed an Epsom horsebox at Six Mile Bottom. Odd, I thought, there was no racing on. Later that night Robert rang me and said that Scobie Breasley had arrived and had been ordered by Tikkoo to take Steel Pulse away. I said, "Let him have a vet's certificate and have him. No arguments."

'When I turned up at Epsom for the Derby, blow me down if Tikkoo didn't come and throw his arms around me like a long-lost friend.'

Armstrong – his superstition is that he will never overtake a funeral hearse – produced good assistants besides Carson and a string of good jockeys. 'Tom Jones started with me. I met him and his father on a boat coming back from Gibraltar. I begged his father to let him be indentured to me. Instead he sent him to Eton – he'd have been better off with me.

'I got him a job in Chantilly but he was back within a week. The owners didn't want a single Englishman in the yard as they were selling a load of horses to England and obviously feared Tom as a spy in their camp.'

Sam was loathe to retire from training but wanted Robert to get the Saint Gatien yard. His one regret is not training a Derby winner. At Haydock Park on 4 November 1972 this outstanding handler saddled his last two runners . . . they both won.

Willie Carson, never sparing in his praise of his former boss, won the first race by five lengths on Raymond Guest's Rag and Des Cullen won the very last race of the season on Ismaquehs. So the last horse Willie rode for Sam was a winner.

Armstrong is a fund of stories. 'I like the one about the new Jewish owner who had a horse with Ron Smyth's father Herbert,' he chuckles. 'Smyth said: "All we need now for you is some colours. I've plenty in my tack room to choose from." Surveying a long line of colours hanging up the newcomer said, "I suppose all these owners are dead." "No," came the quick reply – "broke." '

Sam had the reputation of being a genius with boys, horses . . . and obtaining owners. But he reveals one story against himself which happened on his last day as a licensed trainer at Haydock.

He told me, 'After the second of my two winners had gone in I was keen to dash away as it was a wet day. But as I was about to go off Eric Cousins tugged at my coat sleeve and said, "A man called Robert Sangster would very much like to meet you." I'd never heard of the chap, didn't have a clue who he was, how old, or anything.

'I made the excuse that I had a long journey home and was in a hurry. You never know, I could have met Robert Sangster and had a few horses for him . . . he's certainly done very well.'

And with a knowing smile reflecting fifty years at the top, Sam ponders: 'He was one of the few who got away . . . there weren't many.'

Ironically in the 1977 Derby, two furlongs out it seemed certain that Willie Carson would win on Hot Grove to boost the record of the Armstrong Academy . . . but then along came the famous son-in-law on The Minstrel.

'Both great jockeys,' says Sam, adding, 'I must ring Kipper

Lynch and tell him that he wasn't to blame for Tromos's defeat. He always had him well balanced.'

The Saint Gatien old boys still get a friendly word from their one-time tutor.

Kipper Lynch appreciated Sam's call after the shock defeat of Tromos. He says: 'I was feeling pretty low and a lot of pressmen blamed me rather for the colt's defeat. Sam rang me up and said that I had ridden a perfect race and that it wasn't my fault.

'Sam is a marvellous old man. Willie Carson and all of us have terrific respect for him. He made us work like slaves but he was the making of all of us.

'I remember when Willie came down from the north. He hasn't changed one little bit over the years. He was always the same – so full of bounce. He's so full of go. He's like it when he rides, everything is going.

'Actually it was a lucky switch which took me to Sam Armstrong. My father had fixed me up with a trainer in Epsom. But at the races one day he was told that the trainer wasn't much good and that Mr Armstrong was the best chap for youngsters.

'We wrote to him and that's how I ended up in Newmarket. I had never been to the place before when I arrived to see Sam. I was 4 stone 10 pounds when I rode my first winner on Torque at Brighton in 1956, which was my first-ever ride.

'You don't see 'em that small now. I think that if I saw someone as small as I must have been I'd have a good laugh. Now we look at kids like Wally Swinburn's son Walter, who is about 6 stone 5 pounds and think that he's small. When I started out there were some real titches about.

'When I started with Sam we got sixpence a week, or a shilling if we signed on for seven years. It was a kind of blackmail really – a 50 per cent wage increase if you signed your life away!

'Later our wages rocketed up to half a crown a week. All the lads went on strike and walked out. We wanted five shillings a week. Sam kept the stable going and he and Susan did all the horses. We came back after three days. We got our increase and Sam, who was furious, claimed: "You are silly. You know that you only had to ask."

'Willie and all of us worked hard. Very hard. Sam was cer-

tainly a hard task-master. But we respected him and were prepared to do the hard work. At least we were apprenticed to
somebody who knew the game inside out, and not all lads could
claim that.

'Before any big race Willie and I always walked the course
with Sam. I remember when I won the Great Metropolitan
Handicap at Epsom in 1957 on Geoffrey Brooke's Gay Ballad.

'Sam made Josh Gifford, who rode the favourite Curry, Paul
Tulk and myself walk the complete course – all 2 miles 2 furlongs.

'When we got to the top of the hill Sam said, "Josh, this is
where all the lightweights will drop out. Don't under any circumstances get left in front." Bloody cheek, I thought. He's
talking about me on one of the lightweights. Actually Mr
Brooke had told me two days earlier that I was to attempt to
make all.

'And when we did get to the top of the hill in the race I had
bolted off in front with a 30 lengths' lead – and I wasn't going
back. Gay Ballad broke the course record that day and I don't
think his time will ever be beaten. I slipped the field and stole
the race really. There was no way I should have beaten Curry
as he was a class horse.

'After the race Sam congratulated me and said "Bad luck"
to Josh and Paul Tulk. Later at the yard he said "Well done" to
me. Just as we were all going to bed he said, "Come in here a
minute, Gifford." I listened at the keyhole and heard him give
old Josh a right bollocking. "You bloody fool, Gifford. Fancy
giving that bloody Lynch a 30 length start," fumed Sam. When
Josh came out he chased me all over the yard screaming, "If I
ever get my hands on you, I'll kill you, you little bugger." '

Sam Armstrong trained a winner on every Flat course in
England. He recalls, 'Bath was the last one. Somebody worked
it out that Bath was the only course where I hadn't trained a
winner. Josh Gifford on Curry soon put that right.

'Yes, it's true I do get immense satisfaction from seeing my
ex-boys doing well. Not only the jockeys but some of the people
who went on to become good trainers. There's Tom Jones in
Newmarket, and Chris Thornton, who took over from the late
Sam Hall at Middleham, had a spell with me.

'Miguel Clement came over from France for a time. Sadly he was killed in a car accident when so young. He was a great big man, well over 6 foot. I told him when he arrived, "I haven't got a horse big enough to carry you."

'Years later I met him in France and asked him when he was going to start out as a trainer. He said, "Oh, I shall not start until I've got a hundred horses."

'I couldn't resist telling him that I started out with just one.'

When Willie came south he had just £50 in the world. He says: 'It all went on the down-payment for a caravan. I married Carole who I had met in a Darlington dance hall. The date was 22 January 1962 and I was not yet 20 years old.

'I plucked up courage and asked Mr Armstrong if I could put the caravan in one of his paddocks. I'll never forget the look on his face when the huge caravan arrived.

'Later we moved into a two-up two-down, but it was hard work and I was on only £6 a week. But that was better than when I first moved to Newmarket as I was only on ten shillings. Both the Armstrongs I served were tough masters, real pushers. But I have to thank them for my career as a jockey.'

By the early sixties Carson was regarded as one of the most promising lightweights in the country. He rode five winners in 1963 – his first in Newmarket. Gradually he increased his win totals to fifteen and thirty-seven. The dynamic little apprentice was getting more and more in demand and the youngster, who had lost his allowance at Ripon, was being snapped up by outside trainers.

In 1966 he booted home thirty-five winners. Shrewd eyes were now picking out Willie Carson as a first-class prospect . . . he had even attracted the attention of the man with the most famous name in racing, Lord Derby, and his tuition at the Armstrong Academy was nearly over.

4 'You always have a good laugh with Willie'

Edward John Stanley, the 18th Earl of Derby, is Willie Carson's greatest admirer. He was the man who gave Carson his big chance in racing, and the all-action Scot has often said: 'My biggest ambition is to win the Derby for Lord Derby.'

Carson was the last in a line of distinguished jockeys to be retained as first jockey to Lord Derby. It was the 12th Earl of Derby who planned the first running of the Derby in 1780 during a hearty party at his house. He was a very hospitable man and won the Derby in 1787 with Sir Peter Teazle.

It's ironic that Willie Carson, spotted by the 18th Earl as a future star in the saddle, should win the 200th running of the world's most famous Flat race on Troy. Of course, Willie would love to win the Derby for Her Majesty The Queen – but the present-day Lord Derby would provide a fairy-tale Epsom victory.

John Derby's black Rolls-Royce glides across the paddock-lined Suffolk fenland countryside to Newmarket as he reveals to me exactly how Carson came to be his jockey – a vital switch in his career.

'I was looking for a jockey to succeed Doug Smith as my retained rider,' says Lord Derby. 'Doug was obviously going to retire and I wanted to get fixed up with a new jockey.

'I spent many hours talking over the matter with Bernard van Cutsem, who was then my trainer at Stanley House in Newmarket.

'At that time in 1966 there were two really outstanding young up-and-coming riders – Carson and Sandy Barclay. Bernard used to talk well of Barclay and wanted me to sign him up. I had spotted Carson quite a few times, although when he got the job he had never actually ridden a single horse for me.

'Bernard kept pressing Barclay. I was for ever suggesting that Carson was the man I wanted. Funnily enough, just as we were about to make our decision who to approach the matter was rather taken out of our hands when Sir Noel Murless stepped in and snapped up Barclay.

'I was rather pleased. I'm unashamedly a great Willie Carson fan. I think he's a frighteningly nice little man. He's one of the great jockeys – the complete gentleman. We've never had a cross word.

'He's a natural horseman. I'm still thrilled that I gave him his first real chance in racing. Ever since then his career has jumped on by leaps and bounds.

'He's been very loyal to me. In recent years it has not been worth me retaining my own jockey so Willie is the last of the Lord Derby private jockeys. But he's so good that he will always be available for me if he does not have a stable ride. And he'll always ride out work without getting a penny.'

There is no denying the bond between Lord Derby and Carson. Says Lord Derby as his car pulls into the Jockey Club's Newmarket headquarters: 'Willie remembers when I was loyal to him. He has since repaid my trust in him.

'In those early days at Stanley House I used to run quite a few horses in France. Bernard used to employ Lester Piggott for the big races and I didn't think that it was quite right.

'Lester used to get the good rides. Willie would ride in the less important races and would then be stood down. I told Bernard that as far as I was concerned Willie should ride my horses. It was unfair to give him some rides and then stand him down when a big race came along.

'I liked Willie the moment I met him. You always have a good laugh with Willie.

'Even when he's ridden a lousy, bad horse for you he comes back roaring with laughter. He rode a Sir Ivor colt I had with Willie Hastings-Bass at work one morning. He came back and told me, "I daren't move on him, Sir. It's like sitting on the top of a volcano. There are two things you can do with him . . . run him quick or geld him even sooner. He's got too much life in him."''

Some jockeys would say that Carson has too much life in
him. But it's a super-energy which has made him much loved
in every betting shop in the country. For whenever a horse is
mentioned with Carson on board you can be sure of one thing –
you are on a trier. Racing is always full of stories of jockeys pulling horses. I can think of no rider in racing less likely to 'hook' a
horse up than Willie Carson. It's just not his style.

Willie recalls the evening in July 1966 when Sam Armstrong
called him to his house and said: 'Lord Derby has approached
me about you taking over from Doug Smith as his first jockey.'

Sam recalls: 'It was odd really. Just after the war Bernard
van Cutsem had a few horses with me. He was an extremely
nice man. One day he saw me and said that Lord Derby had
mentioned to him the possibility of me going to Stanley House
as his private trainer. Naturally I was honoured that they
should think of me. But I had just bought Saint Gatien and
Robert was not old enough to take over. I very much wanted to
have my own yard.

'I turned down the offer and it was shortly after that Bernard
van Cutsem took out his own trainer's licence. He was a very
shrewd trainer – and a damned good better. He had the two
most important things for a trainer – lots of patience and plenty
of confidence.

'If things had been different I could have gone to Stanley
House, and the situation of Lord Derby approaching me about
Carson would never have arisen. When the approach did come
I had no hesitation in recommending Carson.

'I told him to think it over for two days. He jokes now that it
took him two seconds.'

Says Carson: 'One day I had a message to go and see Mr
Armstrong. I thought that I was in for another rollicking.

'Instead he told me that Lord Derby wanted me as his
retained jockey the following season. I was very surprised. I
knew that Doug Smith was retiring but I had never ridden a
single horse for Lord Derby.

'I was shaking like a leaf when I went to Stanley House to see
him. But he made me very welcome. I was nervous because I'd
never spoken to a Lord before in my life.'

With the Lord Derby retainer went Falmouth Cottage in the Snailwell Road. So from the neat Newmarket semi-detached house the Carsons were on the move to Falmouth Cottage, for many years the home of Lord Derby's jockey.

Carson was now set to wear the most famous colours in racing . . . the black jacket, white cap and one white button for luck.

The button story began on Derby Day in 1924 when Tommy Weston pulled on the shirt in a hurry, got his white scarf caught through a button hole and went on to win the race on Sansovino.

Yes, there's no doubt that Carson obtained a job absolutely steeped in racing history. Being top jockey to Lord Derby was beyond his wildest dreams.

Actually the famous black jacket started out as green and white stripes. Lord Derby's brother, Richard, who owns the New England Stud at Newmarket which produced Waterloo to win the 1000 Guineas in 1972, has some old pictures of the Derby horses which show clearly the green and white striped silks. Says Richard, a fun-loving character with a zest for life, 'So many people had black colours at the time of 1787 that the 12th Lord Derby decided to change. Later the colours changed back.'

The 12th Earl of Derby was a tremendous party-giver. The whole idea of the Derby was conceived at a dinner-party at The Oaks. It is claimed that Lord Derby and Sir Charles Bunbury tossed up to decide whether the race should be called the Derby or the Bunbury.

Lord Derbys over the years have employed only the best jockeys – Tommy Weston, Harry Wragg, Doug Smith and finally Willie Carson. It's sad that these outstanding patrons of the Turf should see their equine empire wane a little and now there is no need for a retained jockey.

The 12th Earl's real passion was for cock-fighting. One biography calls him 'the greatest cocker who ever lived'. He was well-known for his breeding of black-breasted reds. To the irritation of his wife he often arranged cock-fighting in the drawing-room after dinner.

The Derby home is Knowsley Park, a few miles east of Liverpool. The house began as a shooting lodge in the thirteenth century but was altered by successive Lord Derbys into a huge mansion. There are many paddocks in the 2600 acre walled park, and many of the horses to carry the famous black silks were bred at Knowsley.

The 12th Earl did win the Derby with Sir Peter Teazle in 1787, but then the family, despite constant devotion to the Turf, had to wait for another victory until the 17th Earl won with Sansovino in 1924.

Lord Derby admits that he has an obvious yearning to win the race named after his illustrious forefather. Over the years the home-bred stock of the family has declined, and this is why Willie Carson was the last of the retained riders.

In 1949 Lord Derby was cruelly robbed of a probable victory in the Blue Riband of all races. Doug Smith was on Swallow Tail and the combination hit the front over a furlong out. Then Lady Luck decided to pen the script against the black silks. Swallow Tail was heavily bumped as Nimbus came away from the rail. He was obviously taken out of his stride and by the time he was balanced again the race was over. He was beaten by a head and the same into third place behind Nimbus and Amour Drake. There is no doubt that the bump did cost him the race.

Smith, who rode a winner on every course in England, Wales and Scotland before he was twenty, gave up riding in 1967 at the same time that Geoffrey Brooke retired as a trainer. Smith won several big races for Lord Derby but the vital Derby was not one of them.

He won the Doncaster Cup in 1955 on Entente Cordiale. In 1960 he won the Cesarewitch on Alcove and the Goodwood Stakes the next year on the same horse. Tudor Treasure (St James's Palace at Royal Ascot, 1961) and Latin Lover (Manchester Handicap, 1962) were other big winners for the Lord Derby–Smith team.

Lord Derby is the first to admit that he has not been a lucky owner, although he was fortunate to inherit the outstanding stayer Alycidon, who ironically whipped round at the start of his first race and took no part. Hence he always ran in blinkers afterwards. After being beaten in the St Leger he was never beaten again and won the Cup races as a pastime.

Lord Derby is the senior steward at Aintree, and it was in his private box at the 1979 Grand National meeting that this kindly aristocrat revealed his racing life.

'The breeding side has been a total disaster in recent years,' admits Lord Derby, whose tall, upright figure can always be spotted at the races carrying a black hickory stick.

'Only Broken Record has really made it in the last few years. So often we have bred fillies, one after another. If you have racehorses you can spend a lot of money on the breeding side. It's a mistake really as there are not enough top-class mares about.

'Still in racing things can change. Of course I'd love to win the Derby. I've tried and not been very lucky. Still, you keep on hoping.

'I got my first horse, Stop Press, after he won a seller at Windsor on 4 May 1940. I was stationed at Windsor with the Grenadier Guards. Some friends and I had a bit of a gamble. At the auction I bought Stop Press, but I'm afraid that he turned out to be bloody well useless and he never won.

'As I say I liked Willie the moment I met him. I always call him Willie. My grandfather always called Tommy Weston by his christian name.

'Willie can joke and laugh but he thinks about racing and is a very sound judge. His happy-go-lucky attitude to life is a bit misleading. When High Top was syndicated I was approached. I spoke to Willie and he stressed to me that High Top was a better colt than a lot of people gave him credit for. It was Willie's opinion that made me buy an eighth share and I don't regret that.

'Half the fun of racing is talking over plans with your trainer or jockey. I used to have horses in France. The trainer once ran a horse of mine three times in a week without telling me, and the first I knew of it was when I read the results in the paper. I never sent another horse to France.

'I think the world of Willie. I can't stress how much I admire him. Bernard van Cutsem was also a great Carson fan. Often their opinions differed but Bernard was always very keen to find out what Willie thought.'

Over the years speculation has hinted that Bernard van Cutsem's arrival at Stanley House was not totally unconnected with a game of cards. Lord Derby gives one of his engaging smiles and says: 'Bernard was a very good poker player. At the end of the evening when he got up from the table you never knew whether he had won or lost.'

Lord Derby's great passion in life is golf. 'Ah, there's nothing quite like the American Masters,' he once told me happily after a visit across the Atlantic.

It was on a golf course in Kentucky that Lord Derby learned of his most successful battle with the bookmakers. He recalls: 'I've never been a big punter but I was persuaded to have £200 on Alcove for the Cesarewitch in 1960 at 33–1.

'Actually I got so windy about the bet that I couldn't stay in England. I flew over to play golf in America with some friends. We were out on the course when a chap came running down the fairway to tell me that Alcove had won. We had quite a celebration in the club-house that night, I can tell you.'

If Lord Derby had known what happened at Newmarket it's odds-on that he would have sliced his drive. Alcove, backed down from 8–1 to 100–30 favourite after a win at Nottingham in her previous race, got up by a neck to pip Sea Wolf.

Doug Smith sent her to the front two furlongs out but she wandered and only just saved the day . . . and Lord Derby's bet. Alcove, by Alycidon, never raced for trainer Jack Watts as a two-year-old. She was one of six winning rides in the Cesarewitch for Doug Smith from thirty-one attempts.

Times have changed dramatically since the days of the 12th Earl. His parties at Knowsley Park were such that an author wrote at the time, 'More good ale is drunk there than in any hall in England.'

I wonder if the present Lord Derby's forefathers would have ever expected to see the placard 'Jockey Club and Ladbrokes officials only' at one entrance at Aintree in 1979. As one dry press colleague asked, 'Why have the Jockey Club such an exalted position?'

But Lord Derby is a modern, free-thinking Jockey Club member. Like many a racing man he is superstitious. 'I absolutely hate sitting down to dinner with thirteen people at the table. Won't do it,' he says. 'And if there are four candles on a table I hate to see one taken away. It reminds me of a hearse, with two chaps sitting in the back and one at the foot.'

The 12th Earl had an odd superstition. He refused to have any pianos in Knowsley Park. He had a great dislike of pianos and if he was ever staying away and spotted one he would always lock it up and throw the key into the garden.

'*Sans changer*' – 'without changing' – is Lord Derby's family motto. They are descended from Adam de Audley, who settled in Cumberland in the reign of Henry I.

The motto is appropriate for Lord Derby. Ever since the shy Carson was ushered into Stanley House to be offered his first retainer, Lord Derby has been his greatest admirer . . . without changing.

5 The bionic jockey

Willie Carson had one season as understudy to Doug Smith before he took over as Lord Derby's officially retained jockey at the magnificent Stanley House yard in Newmarket. A long avenue of lime trees screens the stable yards from the busy Bury Road.

The actual stable yard is steeped in history. An impressive clock tower looks down on the boxes where Bernard van Cutsem housed some of the most perfectly bred and expensive horseflesh in the world.

Sadly, Bernard van Cutsem finally lost his long battle against a painful illness in 1975, and racing was robbed of one of its greatest characters. His almost regal personality and non-chalant manner was more suited to a wealthy owner. But he was an extremely shrewd and professional trainer.

Like his main patron, Lord Derby, van Cutsem became an ardent member of the rapidly growing Carson fan club. When Crowned Prince, a record $510,000 yearling, arrived from America in 1971, I visited Stanley House and had a lengthy interview with van Cutsem, who was the British-born son of a Dutch count.

He stressed: 'Willie will be champion jockey one day. He has such a terrific appetite for the game. When Lester Piggott decides to take it a little bit easier and not dash all over the country, Carson is his natural successor. He's a very good rider and being a lightweight gives him a great advantage.'

Van Cutsem was a tall, distinguished figure. Opinions that he was just a socialite playing around with training could not have been more wrong. He had gone to Cambridge University but admitted with a hearty chuckle: 'I only went to one lecture all the time I was there. I was only interested in horses.'

He organized hunter trials, was a keen trainer and rider of his own point-to-pointers, and ran the University Drag. The outbreak of war halted his plans after he had set up as a trainer at Exning, near Newmarket, in 1938. After the war he trained at Graham Place, Newmarket, and it soon became obvious that the attraction of having a tilt at the ring was not unpleasant.

He owned and bred Kalydon, and brought off a wholesale gamble when his Panga was backed off the boards from 20–1 to 9–2 before winning first time out at Newbury. In 1963 he took over the lease of Stanley House, and in 1965 he saddled Lord Derby's Go Shell to win the Portland Plate.

Bernard's greatest moment came when he paid just 500 guineas for a Kalydon filly called Park Top, who was owned by the Duke of Devonshire. Unraced as a two-year-old, she won the Ribblesdale Stakes and three other races as a three-year-old. But it was as a five-year-old that Park Top hit the high spots, winning the Coronation Cup, the Hardwicke and the King George VI and Queen Elizabeth Stakes. As a six-year-old she won La Coupe at Longchamp and the Cumberland Lodge at Ascot before dead-heating in France in the Prix de Royallieu in her farewell appearance.

In 1969 van Cutsem achieved another notable victory when Karabas won the Washington International. Lester Piggott was slammed for his riding of Park Top in the Arc de Triomphe – he came with a late run – but he was masterful on Karabas. The year before he won the Laurel Park race on Sir Ivor, when the American press criticized his tactics. It was after Karabas's win that an American scribe pressed the Long Fella: 'When did you think you'd win?' Lester replied: 'About two weeks ago.'

Mick Ryan, now an established Newmarket trainer well-known for his raids on the Continent for various Derbys, was with van Cutsem for fifteen years, the last three as his assistant.

He told me: 'Bernard used to speak a lot of Willie even before he joined us in 1967. He always said that he'd make a good rider.

'I'm sure that Carson's bionic. He must have plugs in every

night. His will to win is unbelievable. He'll win on anything – and has done.

'When he was with us, if he went two days without a winner he was like a caged tiger. With his low weight he had to be champion jockey one day. He always won on horses that he should have won on.

'But every now and again he would win on horses who simply had no right to win. They were beaten horses until he got to work . . . that's the hallmark of a genius.

'It was obvious when Doug Smith came to the end of his career that Willie was a sound replacement. Russ Maddock didn't quite fit in and anyway he sustained an injury in the Union Jack at Liverpool.

'Willie hasn't changed a lot since those early days. He was always very handy with the stable lads. They liked him – used to call him Prince William. He was well schooled by Sam Armstrong and was always very good in the chats with owners before and after the races.

'He's not devious. Often you hear of jockeys going crock. Not this one, he's very genuine. He was always a perfect servant to the trainer and to the owners.

'I know that he gives the impression of being nonchalant, almost boyish, but he can be serious. He was deadly serious when it came to discussing plans.

'Bernard van Cutsem was a great form-book man. Each night he would burn the midnight oil looking at the handicapping. He was always the last one to bed and usually the first one in the yard.

'The new computer handicapping has taken much of the art of training away. With graded races the job is done for you. But Bernard would spend two or three days studying the Racing Calendar. Often he would pin-point a flaw. He had a rule that he would never run a horse where he was worst in. He always ran them where they were best handicapped.'

Mick Ryan had total respect for van Cutsem. He reflects: 'We called him God. We never thought that he would die. In the stable we just couldn't believe it.

'In the end he was so ill that he had to go into hospital in London. But he still wanted to know everything that was going on. I was in charge of the gallops. I used to tape my immediate reaction to the work the horses had done and then they were taken to Bernard's hospital in London. The last time I saw him he was still asking about the gallops and the entries we had made.

'It was a great blow when he died. We never knew that he was a Roman Catholic until the funeral was arranged.'

Willie Carson admits: 'The guv'nor would have thought nothing of having £1000 on a two-year-old first time if he fancied it.'

Mick Ryan says: 'It used to make me laugh. Sometimes in the parade ring before a race Bernard, who was very tall, would gaze down on little Willie and say, "I've had a few bob on." It was probably more like thousands.'

Van Cutsem used to employ Lester Piggott for the big races. The Long Fella had gone freelance after his bust-up with Sir Noel Murless and was only too keen to partner the Stanley House blue-bloods, many of them expensive purchases in America.

Carson was left to reflect: 'It was the same with Mr Armstrong. I felt that I was just the best lightweight in the yard. Whenever we had anything any good Lester would get the ride. It was obvious as he is the son-in-law.

'At Stanley House I had a great job. But apart from Lord Derby's horses the pick of the rides always went to Lester.'

There is no doubt that Willie thinks to this day that but for the Long Fella his career would have been able to blossom more quickly. So often the tiny Scot lived, and rode, in the shadow of Piggott.

Ryan recalls that Willie was 'very close to van Cutsem'. It's hard to imagine a more unlikely pair than the joke-a-minute Carson and the sombre trainer.

Van Cutsem was not a great after-race talker to the press. He gave a rather aloof impression. His great charm sometimes deserted him when he addressed the racecourse hacks. A classic example came when Willie Carson produced a typical driving finish to win the Royal Hunt Cup at Royal Ascot in 1974 on Old Lucky. Nelson Bunker Hunt's ex-French import had been heavily gambled upon in the ante-post markets from 20–1 down to 8–1 second favourite on the day.

Van Cutsem landed one of his more spectacular coups. When a pressman grabbed his arm and asked, 'What's the plan with this one, Bernard?' he got an icy stare from the trainer and the quick retort: 'That was the plan, you fool.'

Carson says: 'It was a great thrill to wear Lord Derby's colours. I'll never forget that he gave me my big chance. Very early on I promised him that one day I'd win the Derby for him.

'I rode my first winner for him when Robinson Crusoe won a two-horse race called The Whip at Newmarket.

'It was great living at Falmouth Cottage. At first we hardly had enough furniture for the new home. We used to live in corners. I used to imagine Tommy Weston leaving the house before winning the Derby on Hyperion. Doug Smith was also champion jockey five times while he lived there.' Falmouth Cottage was bought by the present Lord Derby's grand-father and named after Lord Falmouth.

Bernard van Cutsem's spacious yard backed on to the Snailwell Road. Under the attractive clock tower there are dozens of racing plates nailed to the wall in memory of the big-race winners from Stanley House. Amongst this array of steel it is easy to pick out the smallest . . . the tiny plate used by the greatest small horse of all-time, Hyperion.

Van Cutsem once told me: 'Willie reminds me very much of Tommy Weston. They were very much alike. Both were rugged little men with strong hands. They both have tremendous strength and determination never to give up. Guts . . . sheer guts.

'I introduced Willie to hunting and now he is crazy about it. I put him on a great 17 hands slab of a horse. He had never jumped anything in his life but I said, "This is your chance," and he took it. He had a couple of tumbles but he just got back on and tried again. He never hesitated once. He is a game one, there is no doubt about that.'

Willie was so smitten with the hunting scene that he bought ex-hurdler Eastern Blaze as his first hunter. He borrowed a full pink-coat from Greville Starkey and really looked the part in the winter sport immortalized by Oscar Wilde as 'the unspeakable chasing the uneatable'.

In 1968 Carson's winners jumped to sixty-one from the previous year's haul of thirty-five. Mick Ryan recalls: 'The great thing about Willie when he rode for us was that he was never downhearted . . . except when he got beat on one. But half an hour later he always bounced back. You'd never knock him down for long.

'He and Bernard were an ideal combination. The trainer always knew which path he was going down. Once he had set out a programme for a horse he never changed his plans in midstream. For his part Willie rode less bad races than most. He never tried to do anything clever or cheeky. If the horses were good enough, they won.'

In 1968 Carson had his first Derby ride. At the age of twenty-six, he first experienced the tension and drama of the world's top Flat race. He donned the famous black silks which Tommy Weston and Harry Wragg had ridden to Derby glory. But for Willie there was to be no fairy-tale victory for his patron.

It was, however, a miracle and a typical piece of Carson's will to overcome insurmountable odds that he was even in the Derby line-up on Lord Derby's Laureate.

At the end of the 1967 season Carson was a happy man as he drove his family north. He had ridden thirty-five winners and was firmly established as Lord Derby's jockey. He also rode for his former guv'nor Sam Armstrong. The security of Falmouth Cottage was a great help.

But in November 1967 – four days after the end of the Flat season – Carson's career lay in ruins amongst the horror spectacle of mangled body-work and tell-tale skid marks on the Great North Road. In dense, swirling fog Carson collided with a wagon which was doing a suicidal U-turn.

Carson's Jaguar was crushed in a second. Amid the shattered metal and glass the last words Willie recalls as he was pulled from the wreckage by ambulancemen were, 'This one's a goner for sure.'

Recalls Willie: 'The next time I came round in hospital I saw a priest standing over me praying for me. That was enough to put me out for the count again.

'The next time I woke up properly I heard the words, "Ten

... twenty ... thirty." It was then that I realized that the nurse was counting the roll of tenners which I had in my back pocket.

'I'm not going to admit how much money there was, but the nurse did joke that it was enough to get her back to her native Jamaica. I laugh about it now but it wasn't very funny at the time.'

Carson's injuries were horrific. He fractured the femur in his right leg and smashed his right ankle, broke his jaw and knocked out his front teeth. He also broke his index finger. He needed thirty-seven stitches in his face. Wife Carole and son Neil suffered from broken thighs, and Carole still has pain from her fractures.

Willie had intended to take his family away for a winter holiday. Instead he spent months in hospital. The following spring as he drove his new Mercedes to van Cutsem's yard for early morning gallops he admitted to me, 'I never thought that one day I'd drive down Newmarket High Street.'

Carson missed the first month of the 1968 campaign. Doctors told him that it was touch-and-go whether he would be back in time for the Derby. They didn't realize the drive and determination inside this 5 foot 1 inch frame.

At the start of the season he was unable to walk, let alone ride. Slowly he started to get about but only with the aid of calipers. Carson was to pass this test of character with flying colours. He was so keen to continue his career and the Stanley House appointment that he amazed doctors by the speed of his recovery.

There was a medical question mark as to whether Carson would be fit in time for the Derby in early June. Instead the cheerful Scot was back in the saddle by early April . . . and back with a bang.

Laureate had run first in the Union Jack Stakes at Liverpool on 28 March. But Carson had to watch the race at home on television. The scars on his face had healed, but his legs were still in calipers. Laureate won easily by four lengths in the hands of Russ Maddock. The win pleased – and frustrated – Willie.

The obvious excitement of having a live Derby hope was

dulled by the frustration of not being able to ride. A telephone call to the doctor resulted in Willie's being told to be patient. Some hopes! Within a few days he persuaded van Cutsem that he was fit enough to work. To the surprise of all the lads he turned up one morning, but van Cutsem was shrewd enough to insist that he only partnered his own hack, Old Dick.

Laureate was slashed from 100–1 to 33–1 for the Derby after the Union Jack Stakes. Willie's big problem, apart from getting back his phenomenal strength, was to lose the few pounds he had put on during the restless winter. Many hours were spent in a sauna he had built in his garden.

Laureate was something of a character, far from easy on the gallops, not perhaps the ideal partner for a jockey trying to ease himself gently back into the routine, but with a natural desire to get on with the job at full throttle. One morning a watcher on the gallops opened up a big black umbrella and Laureate took off across the vast open expanse of the Heath.

On 16 April Willie made his racecourse come-back. It was a tremendous effort to be fit so soon. The memories of the car crash were overtaken by the promise of victories to come as Carson stepped out to ride Bikini at Newmarket in a three-year-old fillies' maiden race. There was no fairy-tale here as Bikini finished tailed off.

Carson had come back too soon. His enthusiasm, great though it was, could not conquer broken bones. His leg pained him, and he was forced to quit race-riding for a spell.

When Laureate ran in the Thirsk Classic Trial on 20 April Russ Maddock kept the ride. Van Cutsem was alert enough to know that despite his keenness, Carson was still not 100 per cent fit. It was also rather unfair to 'jock off' the little Australian, who had ridden the colt to win at Liverpool. Laureate ran in an Australian cheeker, as he was a hard puller.

Laureate was watched by his owner as he was well beaten by five lengths by the northern-trained Chebs Lad. Carson was back on the colt in the Dee Stakes on the ancient Chester course. This time Willie made all and was impressed. The Thirsk defeat could have been put down to restraining the colt and he clearly did not appreciate it when he was hit.

Lingfield's Derby Trial Stakes on 17 May increased Willie's

view that he could well win the Derby at the first attempt . . . and in the colours of Lord Derby. He really fancied that he would fulfil his promise to the owner at the first try.

At half-way Laureate pulled his way to the front. Van Cutsem was insistent that the colt was under no circumstances to be held up. It was one of the first times I noticed the unusual way in which Carson drives a horse out with his hands. He was at the top of the hill but Carson was urging the colt forward as though he was inches from the line in a blanket finish. It was the style which was to drive many a horse into the winner's enclosure when with a lesser jockey on top they would have finished 'out with the washing'.

Staying on well, Laureate beat the favourite Torpid by a length. 'I won easily. He's a funny horse but we are just getting to the bottom of him,' said Carson. Lord Derby and van Cutsem were delighted with the Lingfield running.

Stanley House was a-buzz with speculation that van Cutsem's first Derby victory was just around the corner. Lord Derby admits: 'I did think myself that on that Lingfield showing we had a first-class chance at Epsom.'

Sadly, it was not to be. Laureate finished a far-away eleventh. This was Sir Ivor's golden moment. Lester Piggott came surging past the huge Connaught like a Rolls-Royce surging away from some old crocks.

It was a fabulous display by a class horse. But, oddly enough, years later Lester's father Keith revealed to me: 'It was the worst riding display in a Derby by my son.

'Lester had won on Joe Mercer's mount Remand as a two-year-old and was convinced that he would win the Derby. All through the race he watched Joe Mercer and was determined to challenge when he did.

'Suddenly he realized that Joe was going backwards and he had to make a sudden spurt to the leaders. Then, in all truth, he beat Connaught, who did not really stay.

'It may have looked a brilliant bit of riding but actually Sir Ivor let Lester off the hook. He was watching the wrong one.'

Pipe-puffing Joe Mercer had seen so many of his Derby dreams go up in smoke. By 1979 he'd had twenty-six Derby rides and could only boast seconds on Fidalgo (behind his father-in-law Harry Carr on Parthia in 1959) and Relkino (1976).

Mercer recalls: 'I really fancied Remand. But suddenly every horse in Dick Hern's yard started coughing. From Chester onwards everything went wrong. Remand seemed to be OK, but when I went out to the paddock before the Derby I couldn't recognize him. He'd gone as well and I didn't have a cat in hell's chance.'

At the top of the hill Carson had moved into third place on Laureate, who had sweated up slightly in the lengthy and tension-filled pre-parade. It was half-way down Tattenham Corner that Connaught took it up with Sandy Barclay on board. Carson was ideally placed just half a length behind the leader.

As the field swung into the straight it was easy to see Lord Derby's black colours in second place. Indeed Carson said afterwards: 'I was working very hard to prevent Laureate pulling his way to the front too soon. I was feeling very confident at that stage.'

But suddenly Carson's dream of a first Derby win at the initial attempt was over. And for Lord Derby and van Cutsem there was no mistaking the disappointment which their binoculars all too clearly pin-pointed.

Laureate's challenge died in a few strides as though he had been shot. Three furlongs out he dropped his bit, and at the finishing post only the backmarkers Benroy and First Rate Pirates were behind him of the thirteen runners.

Piggott won by 1½ lengths on Sir Ivor and the below-par Remand was a tragic fourth for luckless Mercer and his trainer Dick Hern. The West Ilsley trainer's Derby luck was not to change for another eleven years . . . and then it was to be with Carson as jockey, giving a brilliant, never-say-die riding performance.

Lord Derby smiled at Carson and said, 'Never mind.' Yet again he had the torture of another flop in the one race he yearned to win. Carson said at the time: 'For a few seconds I had the joyous feeling that I was on a Derby winner as Connaught and Laureate led the field into the straight. It was a lovely feeling.

'He stopped nearly dead and Lester went past us with a bang. Now, not unnaturally, I'm even more keen to win the race in Lord Derby's colours.'

Mick Ryan was not a great Laureate fan and the Derby defeat did not altogether surprise him. He recalls: 'Some of Lord Derby's horses at that time rather flattered to deceive. He was a shade feminate. I'm not saying that he was ungenuine but he was not robust enough. But at Liverpool, Chester and Lingfield, when it was his day, you'd have to say that he was a good horse.

'Racing at that time was changing. Sir Ivor was a typical American-bred colt. Competition in the breeding game suddenly became very intense, and even patrons like the late Lord Rosebery and Lord Derby couldn't really compete and their horses deteriorated.'

Van Cutsem was also not totally surprised by Laureate's defeat. He said sadly afterwards: 'He chucked it.' In his next race, the Princess of Wales's Stakes at Newmarket, Carson was told to make all the running on Laureate. But he did not pull this time and after finishing last Willie reported: 'He was never going a bit.' Laureate never raced again and a subsequent test on a cardiograph showed that he had a weak heart.

If he had enjoyed the same bounce and energy as his pilot he could have been a very good horse . . . and perhaps even made all the Derby dreams come true for Stanley House connections.

6 'Home and wet' on High Top

High Top, led out of the Houghton sales ring at Newmarket when he failed to reach his reserve as a yearling, gave Willie Carson his first Classic success in 1972. He was an appropriate winner of the 2000 Guineas for the all-action jockey.

For High Top had always lived and galloped in the shadow of Bernard van Cutsem's staggeringly expensive American-bred 'wonder horse' Crowned Prince. As with the Piggott–Carson situation at Stanley House, High Top was the rather unfashionable back-up representative.

At the start of the 1972 campaign Crowned Prince was 6–4 favourite to win the Guineas. 'Ridiculous price. I hope nobody has been mad enough to back him at that price,' van Cutsem told me in the spring. 'Anybody who has wants putting in a mental home.' Apart from being very much an establishment figure the talented trainer was also a fierce Tote monopolist.

Crowned Prince had flopped at 7–2 on his first racecourse debut. But wearing blinkers he won the Champagne Stakes at Doncaster to save his reputation. In the Dewhurst at Newmarket Piggott scored an impressive victory, and Classic hopes were high at the start of 1972.

But Newmarket's Craven Stakes proved conclusively that Crowned Prince was not going to rule the Classic scene. Starting at 9–4 on he struggled to be a distant fourth. Van Cutsem's world had fallen apart, and he hardly appreciated one rather insensitive colleague of mine who dashed up to him in the gloomy runners-up enclosure and said, 'You surely won't run him in the Guineas after that, will you Bernard?' The crestfallen trainer did not answer.

Little could van Cutsem have realized that within four weeks he would indeed be in the winner's enclosure after the 2000 Guineas, and Carson would have opened his Classic account. At deserted Yarmouth racecourse Crowned Prince and Piggott had a farewell gallop. The massive colt went badly and van Cutsem flew to Sandown later that day to announce: 'He won't run again. We think that he has a soft palate.'

The stage was now set for High Top to gain mammoth consolation for van Cutsem. High Top, who had the feared four white socks, had been bought privately by van Cutsem on behalf of electronics tycoon Sir Jules Thorn for a giveaway 9000 guineas.

While the world watched Piggott and Crowned Prince in his two-year-old career, Carson and High Top won three of their four juvenile races. His only defeat came when he failed to give 3 pounds to Yaroslav in the Washington Singer Stakes at Newbury. He was given 2 pounds less than Crowned Prince in the Free Handicap after putting up his best display when winning the Observer Gold Cup from Steel Pulse.

Carson and High Top made an ideal combination. Piggott had the glamour with Crowned Prince. The former duo were rather more unfashionable . . . but with bags of guts.

High Top showed his successful transformation to a three-year-old in the Yellow Pages Classic Trial at Thirsk. Carson made every inch of the running on the Derring Do colt and ran out an easy 5 lengths winner. Well behind him that day was the filly Waterloo, who went on to win the 1000 Guineas. So Thirsk was the unlikely venue for the two Guineas winners to appear.

Another van Cutsem Guineas hope went out of the window when Piggott finished second on Sharpen Up, a warm 6–5 favourite, in the Greenham. There were no outstanding colts about, and by sheer out-and-out galloping ability High Top started as 85–40 favourite for the Guineas.

'Home and wet,' was gleeful Carson's post-race quote after he had driven High Top from pillar to post in driving rain. At half-way I remember thinking that High Top was going to be one of the easiest Guineas winners for years. Carson and High Top seemed to love bowling along in front.

The driving rain and wind did not seem to worry High Top,

but suddenly Bill Williamson, a delightful little Aussie sadly no longer with us, unleashed a terrific challenge on the Vincent O'Brien-trained Roberto. It seemed that Roberto would get up to pip the front-runner.

But not for the first nor last time we were to witness a stubborn refusal by Carson to surrender. Producing a typical, powerful finish, he kept High Top going for a half-length victory.

Carson said: 'We were in front very soon. He loves to bowl along on his own. I saw Roberto coming at us in the last furlong but High Top quickened a bit and was always holding his challenge.'

Van Cutsem was clearly delighted but he was quick to point out, 'At home Crowned Prince used to murder High Top. But naturally I'm very pleased that all has gone well today.'

Ironically Roberto, aided by an unforgetable Piggott ride, went on to win the Derby. High Top never won again.

Carson was 11–8 on to win the Irish Derby but flopped badly into seventh place behind Paddy Prendergast's shock 33–1 winner Ballymore, who had never been on a racecourse before. Then in the Sussex Stakes he started 11–10 on in a three-horse race and was pipped by a head by Sallust. Then he lost by a nose to Lyphard in the Prix Jacques Le Marois at Deauville. When he finished fourth behind Sallust and Lyphard in the Prix du Moulin du Longchamp in the autumn High Top's racing career was over.

He was not entered for the Derby and was simply trained to the second to gallop his rivals into the ground at Newmarket on Guineas day. After that, like most of the van Cutsem hopefuls, his form fell away and he was clearly not the same horse.

Van Cutsem's then-assistant, Mick Ryan, recalls: 'I think we got the first real outbreak of the wretched virus so common now. At that time we did not suspect that a virus could have such an affect on the horses. You could not blame the soft palate for all the out-of-form horses. Crowned Prince's weight absolutely fell away.

'By the Irish 2000 Guineas High Top was just not right. He did not run within stones of his form. In the English Guineas we were lucky that he was able to set a good gallop. Bernard and Willie had agreed that we knew he was a good galloper. Bernard's last instructions were, "Let's see what he can do. Make all."

'High Top was much better than people realized. He was never quite right after that. He was terrible in Ireland and then he never got the ground he wanted. But he battled back and was never disgraced.'

Lord Derby was soon pressed by Carson to buy a share in the colt. He says: 'Willie insisted that High Top was a much better colt than his form suggested. It was purely because of his advice and encouragement that I bought an eighth share. I certainly don't regret it. In 1977 his daughter Triple First won the Musidora at York, the Nassau Stakes at Goodwood and then the Sun Chariot Stakes at Newmarket.' Another of High Top's relatives who turned into a good sort was his full half-brother Camden Town, who was third in the William Hill Dewhurst Stakes in 1977 when trained by Peter Walwyn.

It was in 1971 that Willie Carson first challenged Lester Piggott for his championship. Lester ended with 162 winners but Willie was not far behind with 145. Since he obtained the Lord Derby retainer his winners had increased yearly from sixty-one to sixty-six and on to eighty-six. Then in 1971 he joined the top bracket.

Piggott first became champion in 1960 and, after losing the title to Scobie Breasley for three seasons, he resumed at the top from 1964 onwards. The Long Fella was the king of the jockeys. No questions asked on that score. Of course not even Lester could match the record of Sir Gordon Richards, later to be closely associated with Carson, who was champion for twenty-six years in all and but for an accident at Salisbury in May 1941, when he broke a leg, would have enjoyed a run of twenty-three consecutive titles.

Carson's immense strength from his small frame was beginning to be displayed everyday on the tracks. His great advantage over Piggott was his ability to ride at a stone less. By 1970 Willie was chalking up a staggering 699 rides. On the basis of a race being a mile it meant that Willie rode from London to Edinburgh and back again in the year!

There was no boasting from Carson. His modesty has

always been one of his most pleasant characteristics. Indeed before the 1972 campaign he said: 'Unless Lester goes off to France for two months in the middle of the season I've no chance of being champion.

'I don't think I will be champion. Don't forget that Lester is always able to pinch the best horses. All the time he wants to be champion the title is his.'

It was around this time that Piggott did in fact spend more time on the Continent. Carson refused to see himself as Lester's successor. He claimed, 'By the time Lester goes, somebody else will probably come along. To be honest I'd rather win the Derby – that's more my style.'

Willie burst on to the big-race scene when he won the 1968 Northumberland Plate – the pitmen's Derby – on Lord Derby's Amateur. At 100–9 he landed a good gamble for van Cutsem.

Laureate had been a big Derby disappointment as Willie's initial ride in 1968, and he was unplaced in 1971 and 1972 on Meaden and Meadow Mint.

The 1972 season started with Lester 4–5 to retain his title, but the bookies were giving nothing away and Carson was 6–4 with his great pal Tony Murray rated a 4–1 shot. There is no doubt that Willie felt that the existence of Piggott was proving something of a stumbling-block to his career. A good example was the horse Golden Monad. Willie rode a blinder on him to win on Lincoln Day in 1971. Ironically it was Lester who was beaten by a length on the runner-up Frances Louise. Then the duo went on to floor the odds laid on Domineering in the Dee Stakes at Chester. Then came one of a series of 'jockeying-off' blows which the little Scot was forced to suffer.

When Golden Monad runs in the £11,742 Prix Henry Delamere at Longchamp in September, it's no other than Lester who is in the saddle and pockets the winning prize-money percentage. As Willie observed at the time: 'Lester takes rides whenever and wherever he wants them. It makes it very hard for the rest of the boys.' The 'LP' obtaining-rides saga has been playing for many years. His close friend Charles St George sums up one point of view by saying, 'I want Lester because he is the best. What's wrong with wanting the best?' Fair comment. But it has made life difficult for several top jockeys – notably Willie Carson, Tony Murray and, to a lesser extent, Ernie Johnson.

Van Cutsem had become a total Carson devotee. He told me before the 1972 season: 'He is nearly as good as Lester. If Lester does take things easy, Willie will be champion. No doubt about it.'

The Stanley House trainer was dead right about the outcome. But one story relates that he wasn't always quite on the ball. Richard Onslow, now racing's leading historian with so many books that he had to move house to accommodate them, was based in Newmarket at this time. He was enjoying a glass of beer in the Subscriptions Rooms when van Cutsem beckoned him over. In his usual forthright way van Cutsem said, 'I'm extremely displeased with you. I am a professional trainer like Jarvis and Rochford. I notice that you continue not to report the gallops of my horses. My owners and I are very annoyed. Unless you do report the work gallops I shall sue you and the editor of the *Sporting Life*. Have you anything to say?' Richard countered: 'Only that I work for the *Sporting Chronicle*.' A slightly embarrassed van Cutsem quickly offered the grinning scribe another drink.

Willie's champion season started at an unlikely venue . . . Naas in Ireland. Before the start of the English campaign the go-anywhere-for-a-winner jockey teamed up with the Ted Curtin-trained Ascertain to win the Fishery Maiden Stakes. It was a neck victory in Nelson Bunker Hunt's world-famous colours, and typically it needed all the Carson flair to get up on the line.

He missed out on the opening Doncaster meeting but kicked home his first winner in England when Bernard van Cutsem landed a good gamble with Baragoi at Leicester. The Carson cavalcade of winners was on the move. By Royal Ascot he had a clear lead over Tony Murray, and it became obvious that Lester was not going to chase for the championship. Willie shared the top-jockey honours at Royal Ascot in a four-way tie with Piggott, Joe Mercer and Ron Hutchinson. Then he rounded off a great week by completing a treble at Redcar on the Saturday on Ennis Mail, Song of the Sea and Monhegan.

Ennis Mail was a chance ride for Carson as Ray Still arrived too late. Willie was already having that little bit of luck that all champions so desperately need.

Tony Murray, a close friend of Carson, said: 'Willie is bound to be champion. He has that terrific weight advantage.' Carson, as he does today, kept up the relentless search for winners. Many weeks he travelled over 3000 miles, and for nine months did not have a single day off. Being champion jockey is no easy task.

Perhaps Willie's will to win was getting him into similar unfortunate scrapes like the young Piggott. In June Willie was stood down for four days after finishing third on Prosper at Yarmouth. There was no camera patrol but the stewards found that Willie had caused interference. It was his first ban since the previous season, when he suffered three days' suspension for his riding of Hitesca in the Esher Cup at Sandown.

Willie had eighty-one winners by 29 July with Murray, sidelined briefly by injury, on seventy. Bookies, always a shrewd gathering of gentlemen, knew which way the game was going, and made Carson 9–4 on and Murray 11–4.

But another ban for Carson meant that the pressure was on him. He was suspended by the Goodwood stewards for seven days after the stewards found that he had caused interference on Dancing Gypsy in the seller. Ironically Murray won on Angel Aboard.

It was a bad day for Carson. He put up 2 pounds overweight on Hardy Scot in the Extel Centenary Handicap and after making all the running on the favourite was pipped on the line by Warpath and his remarkable, fifty-five-year-old jockey from the north, Alec Russell.

But there was no stopping Carson. He was riding at so many meetings and so many races that he could even overcome a run of forty-seven consecutive losers.

After the Goodwood ban he was soon back at his brilliant, driving best. At Nottingham on his first day back he pulled off a 503–1 treble. Windy Bank was his first winner and Carson pipped his rival Murray into second place. His second winner was for Bill Wightman on Major Tory. Quipped the Hampshire trainer: 'If Willie can win on this horse he deserves to be

Luckless Dibidale and Carson gallop on in the 1974 Epsom Oaks . . . but all to no avail. The saddle had slipped and Carson gave a superb bareback riding display, but could not weigh in correctly

Left: A very special owner . . . Willie Carson with The Queen at Newmarket in 1978

Below left: The one Carson rejected – Milford. Willie may have preferred Troy in the Derby, but here they're a winning team in the William Hill July Cup at Newmarket in 1979

Below: . . . and Lord Porchester and Willie are clearly delighted

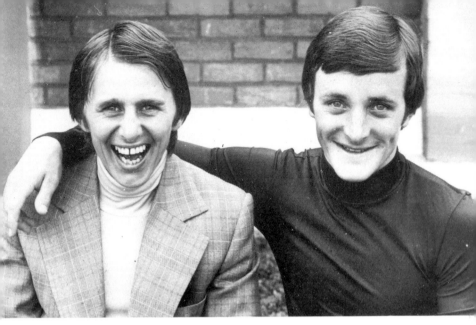

Willie and Pat Eddery don't look like deadly rivals – and they aren't unless they are under starter's orders

The battle of Newmarket, 1975. Willie struggles with striking stable lads before being dragged from Pricet and struck with his own whip

the champion.'

By August Carson had really struck form. He had achieved the first century of his career when winning on Brother Somers at Haydock Park on 20 August the previous season. Now he breezed by this total much earlier. All was well for Willie until he partnered Tritherm for Clive Brittain in the Sancton Maiden Stakes at York on 30 August. The race was won by subsequent Derby runner-up Cavo Doro, but Carson met with a serious injury.

Five furlongs out Tritherm unseated Carson and he crashed to the ground. It was a horror fall. Carson was rushed to York County Hospital with a fractured cheekbone, a cracked wrist and a swollen right eye. Carson was badly shaken up but he said: 'The pain from my injuries was nothing compared to the sinking feeling in my stomach at that moment. Doctors told me that I would be out for six weeks. Imagine it – six weeks. I could say goodbye to any title chances.'

Yet again Lady Luck took a hand against Carson. Murray stepped in to take over two of Willie's mounts and landed a double. That made the score just 105 to 101 in Carson's favour. Bookies quickly made Murray 6–4 on to be the champion. They didn't bargain on the grim determination inside the badly bruised frame in the York County Hospital.

It was Willie's friend Ted Eley who put the spark back into the unwilling patient. He told him at the hospital that night about Murray's double. Carson decided not to scratch his rides for the following week. An amazing action by a man supposed to be sidelined for six weeks.

Two days of agonizing hot and cold water compresses with specialist Bill Tucker in London put Willie on the mend. The doctors in York must have got a shock when they read the race-card for the evening meeting at Windsor the following Monday. The man for whom they had forecast six weeks of inactivity was back in the saddle in four days. He defied the doctors . . . and won by 20 lengths on Parnell for van Cutsem. What a come-back!

'A match made in heaven,' is how Mick Ryan recalls the Parnell–Carson combination. He says: 'They were like two peas in a pod. Guts was their password. They were small but they had hearts like buckets. I can't think of a horse and a jockey being more compatible.'

By the first week of November the championship race was over. At Newbury on 1 November Carson completed a double for van Cutsem on Play Bach and White to Move – the stable's last two runners of the season. It took his score to 131 – nine in front of Tony Murray. The eight-year reign of King Lester was over. Said Lester, 'Naturally I am sorry to lose the title but Willie has earned it by sheer determination.' Carson said: 'I am very happy to win the championship from perhaps the greatest jockey of all time.'

Ironically, one of the horses to win and virtually tie up the championship for Carson was Tritherm, the horse who had clipped another colt's feet when falling at York. The combination had a happier time when winning at Nottingham. Willie finally beat Murray 132 to 125.

At Haydock on the final day of the season as the autumn leaves fluttered to the ground, Carson won on Rag for Sam Armstrong, who went on to complete a double with Ismaquehs. They were the last winners Sam trained before he handed over the reins to his son Robert.

Carson's win total was in fact down on the previous year of 145, when he finished second to Piggott. The virus outbreak had crippled van Cutsem's yard for several weeks, and this did affect his total number of rides and winners.

Murray was gracious in defeat. He overcame a terrible fall himself at Windsor some years back. Now he was, as Willie put it, 'my closest friend, biggest rival.' Said likeable Murray: 'More than anything else Willie is champion because he never gives up. There have been times when I've been finishing almost last in a race and I've seen some mad-man riding the ears off his mount to pass me and finish a bit closer. That's always Willie. He'd rather finish sixteenth than seventeenth.'

Carson had ridden 365 more races than Piggott and ridden twenty-nine more winners. Murray had to suffer a bad patch, when after The Admiral won at Haydock on 29 September he did not win again until 16 October. His stable of Ryan Price at Findon virtually closed down because of the firm ground.

Willie was a reluctant champion in many ways. He realized

that Piggott was still regarded as the supreme jockey. At his home the next spring Willie did insist: 'I may be the champion but Lester is still the king. It's like boxing: Joe Frazier is the world heavyweight champion at the moment but everybody knows that Muhammad Ali is really the best fighter.'

But Carson had broken into the Classic scene on High Top and was now champion jockey. High Top had overcome the worst draw of the lot in the Guineas – number 13 on the far outside. Carson had overcome the York crashing fall.

He had at last escaped the shadow of Lester. As Willie once said: 'He had been on my back for so long. I seemed doomed to play second fiddle to him for life. At Sam Armstrong's he used to get the best rides because he was the son-in-law. When I went to Bernard van Cutsem I was only number one rider for one owner, Lord Derby. I missed out when it came to the others and the big races, like Park Top in the King George VI and Karabas in the Washington International. Still I was lucky in that Lester was contracted to ride Crowned Prince and he had palate trouble, and I was able to ride High Top to win the Guineas.'

High Top was rated by Carson at that stage as the best horse he had ridden for obvious reasons. But van Cutsem always claimed that Parnell was the best horse he ever trained. He had won the Irish St Leger when trained in Ireland. He came to Newmarket as a four-year-old and put up a terrific performance with Willie in the saddle when second, beaten by just 1½ lengths, behind the fabulous Brigadier Gerard in the King George VI.

After his easy Windsor win he was rated a good hope for lifting the Arc de Triomphe. He gave Carson a good first ride in the Paris thriller but weakened towards the end and finished ninth behind San San.

He also provided Willie with his first ride in America. Sadly, unlike the previous van Cutsem raider Karabas, Parnell was not successful. He did, however, run a blinder and was second to Droll Role. I went over for the Laurel Park race that year. It was highlighted by talkative Irish-based jockey Buster Parnell's description of the track. He reckoned that there was a big hole on the far side and this resulted in his mount, Boreen, falling. He also brought down Lester Piggott on Jumbo Jet, who had a very lucky escape.

My biggest memory of Carson in his first season as champion was his ride on King Top in the year's last big handicap, the Manchester Handicap at Doncaster. It was sheer poetry to see Carson win on the John Oxley-trained King Top. Lesser men would have accepted defeat from a hopeless position. But Carson, with typical head-down style, went flying past horse after horse and as if spurred on by a demon, just got up on the line to win by a head and a head. It was a breathtaking performance. The power of wee Willie never ceased to amaze me. Such is his determination and grit that I'm sure, despite his lack of inches, that he'd make an Olympic weightlifter.

The season was over and Carson relaxed . . . by riding out with the morning and afternoon hunts of the Quorn at Hungerton in Leicestershire. He also rode in Kenya, Africa and Rhodesia. With him on the trip was Tony Murray.

Carson, always a generous host, was left with one pleasant task – to organize a party to celebrate his championship win. At Shelford's Uplands Hotel he invited his friends to share his win. Frankie Durr made a speech and said: 'Congratulations to Willie. You are a credit to your profession. May you be champion for many years to come.' Willie received a case of 1846 Madeira wine. Explained Michael Wilson, owner of the Uplands: 'The first recorded champion was E. Flatman in 1846 with eighty-one winners. I was lucky to find a case of the same year.'

The year of 1972 had been a vintage one for Willie. Being champion did not change his happy-go-lucky outlook on life. Indeed as the champagne corks popped amongst the little men, he told his fellow jockeys: 'A friend from Texas once gave me a ten-gallon hat. I am leaving it at the front door and all contributions will be gratefully received.'

After eight years of poker-faced Piggott this was the era of the very contrasting joking champion.

7 'I'm only happy when I'm riding winners'

Bernard van Cutsem noticed that a letter his butler handed him had come from a top London hotel. Its anonymous message was a simple one . . . 'Get rid of Carson before I shoot him.'

The aristocratic van Cutsem often used to chuckle when recalling that story. He said: 'I was amazed that it should come from someone who was staying in an exclusive London hotel. He asked why I should employ such an idiot jockey.

'It was funny really because Willie has always been as straight as a Roman road. He'd be the last jockey to hook one up. On the contrary, he wins on horses which strictly have no right to win.'

At the outset of the 1973 season Willie was the champion. But just two fears haunted the little Scot . . . the threat of the sniper's bullet and the colour of green.

Like all jockeys Willie is superstitious, and a dread of the colour green is high on the list of fears. Before the start of the season I visited Willie at his home and he revealed: 'I absolutely hate the colour of green. It's terribly unlucky in racing. Most owners steer well away from it.

'I've had green suits and shirts but I won't wear them at any price.' I was interested when former jump champion jockey Ron Barry revealed to me another rider's fear . . . that of wearing brand-new colours or silks. 'We always trample them on the floor and get them a little dirty,' said big Ron in that Limerick-Penrith brogue which is so difficult to understand, so difficult at times that when he rode for fun-loving Hawick trainer Ken Oliver, the 'Benign Bishop', as he was dubbed, used to tell him on the telephone: 'For God's sake speak

English, man!'

As champion Carson was in demand in the winter through-out the world. He rode in India, and on one occasion had to show his quickness of movement. He recalled: 'The war with Pakistan was at its height while I was out in India riding that winter. Just as I was leaving the hotel to make my way to the airport there was an air raid.

'Arkle could not have cleared the wall I jumped better. I really flew over it and just missed a terrific explosion.'

Back in England just before the start of the Flat, Carson was soon in the hunting fields with the famous Quorn and Cottes-more packs in Leicestershire. It was Bernard and his wife Mimi van Cutsem who introduced Willie to hunting.

Willie used to ride Mimi's enormous 17 hands chaser, Jolly's Clump, who later became a strong Grand National hope. Most men who rode around 7 stone 10 pounds, would have been put off by the prospect of riding such a huge beast, but not Carson.

'I had some wonderful days,' he said. 'One afternoon we never stopped galloping and jumping. It was tremendous.' Such was Willie's love of the hunting fields and Jolly's Clump that we used to sneak away to tiny jump-race meetings to see the horse in action in hunter chases.

But when the 1973 Flat season loomed ahead and the van Cutsem blue-bloods were being prepared for their campaign, the Newmarket trainer insisted that Carson was not in the hunt. Van Cutsem quite correctly decided that the risk of his champion jockey's being injured hunting was too much and banned him.

You could hardly blame the trainer. Carson has never done anything by halves and there was a real risk of injury. At this stage Stanley House was looking to several colts and fillies to continue the Classic-winning form of High Top the previous season.

Top of the list were two useful colts, Noble Decree and Ksar. In the previous year's Observer Gold Cup Carson had suffered an unpleasant jolt to his assessment of horse-power. Lord Rotherwick's Ksar had greatly impressed Willie when he slaughtered twenty-four rivals by four lengths in the Westley Maiden Stakes at Newmarket on 30 September.

Carson had already won on Nelson Bunker Hunt's Noble Decree at Newmarket in July, but had finished second on the same colt in Ascot's Royal Lodge Stakes. Willie was left with the decision of which horse to ride in the Observer Gold Cup, the Flat's last big two-year-old pre-Classic pointer. Willie picked the wrong one . . . and had the double blow of handing a valuable winner to his arch rival Lester Piggott.

In a desperate finish Piggott got up by half a length on Noble Decree to pip Ksar. Willie seemed certain to endorse his judgement but the Long Fella, who had been last into the straight, came with a typical run to get up on the line.

The van Cutsem yard had the entire winter to ponder which was the better of these two colts. Ksar showed that he had trained on well as a three-year-old when he came out and turned the Sandown Classic Trial into a 5 length procession. But Noble Decree was a disappointing 6–4 favourite when only fourth in the Classic Trial at Kempton.

Van Cutsem decided to run Noble Decree in the 2000 Guineas and put Ksar by as his Derby hope. Noble Decree was American-bred and by the Arc de Triomphe hero, Vaguely Noble. Ksar, an impressive chestnut, was by the late Kalydon. Training first and second in the Observer was a great feat – especially as the Observer was always a sure-fire guide to the following season's Classics.

The race was full of subsequent Classic winners. Vaguely Noble had won the Observer in 1967, and in 1971 High Top had won for van Cutsem prior to his 2000 Guineas success.

Now Noble Decree and Carson were out to repeat High Top's win. They failed by only a head. Willie rode 18–1 Noble Decree to perfection, and when they hit the front over one furlong out it seemed that the same yard was going to strike again. Frankie Durr on 50–1 no-hoper Mon Fils had attempted to do a High Top. He had gone to the front, determined to let his stamina take its full advantage. When collared by Carson inside the final furlong Mon Fils seemed beaten but he came again and just got his head in front bang on the line.

'I've got a meal ticket for life,' said Mon Fils's trainer Richard Hannon, who was tasting Classic success for the first time. The previous evening I had dined at the same country pub as Hannon and his owners. The likeable young East Everleigh trainer made no secret that he fancied Mon Fils. I must admit that I thought at the time that he had lost his senses. Next morning Richard bought a new suit in Newmarket. 'I suddenly thought, God, you can't turn up in the winner's enclosure after the 2000 Guineas wearing this tatty old suit,' he recalls.

Ironically, Mon Fils and Noble Decree never won again. Carson's hopes now turned to the Derby and Ksar. The Lingfield Derby Trial, won by van Cutsem and Carson with Laureate, was now the next target for Ksar. He started at 13–8 on favourite but hardly won in that style. It was a desperate struggle from the home turn before Willie got up by half a length to beat Geoff Baxter on Projector.

It became clear that this was not an outstanding year for three-year-old colts and the Derby would not take a great deal of winning. The day before Ksar's win at Lingfield we had seen a hitherto unraced three-year-old called Morston make a winning debut. A half-brother to Derby winner Blakeney, he was spotted by some shrewd judges as a likely Derby winner. Arthur Budgett begged Geoff Lewis to ride Morston, but he couldn't rustle up any of his usual enthusiasm for the Lingfield maiden winner. Edward Hide eventually had the ride. When he walked into the Epsom paddock he had never seen Morston before. 'Don't hit him. Just do your best,' was kindly Budgett's advice.

Carson had the choice again between Ksar and Noble Decree. Unlike the Observer Gold Cup he went for the right one, but there was to be no fairy-tale ending.

Ksar was the medium of a terrific gamble at the last minute. His price was clipped from 7–1 to 5–1 favourite. Punters realized that it was probably a sub-standard Derby. Guineas first and second, Mon Fils and Noble Decree (ridden by Brian Taylor), were next in the betting at 11–2 and 9.

Carson picked Ksar but then suffered an injury which would probably have put lesser mortals out of the Epsom line-up. At Warwick a horse called Second Hall, ridden by Joe Mercer, kicked out and Carson's right ankle was injured.

Willie in 1973 became a columnist for the *Sun*. So a week

before the Derby he was able to give readers the good news. He said: 'Wonderful news! My London specialist has given me a first-class ticket to ride again.

'My right ankle has recovered so it's full steam ahead for the Derby.

'The specialist examined my chipped ankle and told me I will be fit in time for the Derby. The knock had aggravated an old injury which I received in that terrible car crash five years earlier. Missing the Derby would have been a big blow. I was worried stiff when the Warwick ambulancemen carried me away. At one stage it looked hopeless but the medical people have done wonders.

'Ksar? I'm aware that I've never even been placed in the Derby and I'd love to win. It's my main ambition in life. I'm sure that if the ground is firm and they go a good gallop, Ksar will be in there at the death.

'Much has been made of my choice of Ksar rather than Noble Decree, who has Classic form. Certainly Noble Decree has a better turn of speed. But Ksar has more speed than people imagine. Ksar's big quality besides his consistency and genuineness is that he is a good galloping horse.'

It's history now how Edward Hide won on Morston, who was running only the second race of his life. Ksar's lack of finishing speed was to prove fatal to his Derby chances. Two furlongs out Carson struck the front on Ksar and a mighty cheer went up. His 5–1 favouritism was a reflection of the public's faith in the dynamic little pilot on board.

But no sooner had Carson gone to the front than the one big fear about Ksar came true. In a few strides his chance was lost as Morston, Cavo Doro and Freefoot flashed by. Ksar finished fourth and was like Laureate an obvious disappointment to Carson. Twice he now knew the thrill of leading a Derby field – and the agony of seeing the big prize snatched away. Ironically Noble Decree finished twenty-fourth of the twenty-five runners. Only Satingo finished behind Noble Decree and he was never to race again. He was immediately sent to stud.

Carson had clearly got the Ksar–Noble Decree chances correct this time. Years later when faced with the Troy–Milford problem, one commentator said, '. . . and here comes Willie

Carson on Troy. He picked the wrong one once before but he hasn't this time.' Willie, never shy to correct a wayward scribe, was quick to point out the error. Ksar had finished fourth, Noble Decree twenty-fourth.

In his column Carson predicted that the Oaks was 'nothing Mysterious'. Noel Murless's outstanding filly duly won the Oaks by four lengths, but Willie was in the cash as he finished third on Aureoletta for Barry Hills. It was not to be a lucky race for the Hills–Carson duo. This was Willie's second Oaks ride. In 1972 he had been unplaced on van Cutsem's Austria.

By 1973 Carson had established himself. More and more of van Cutsem's owners began to appreciate the muscle-power of Carson. The shadow of the Long Fella did not loom so menacingly over the choice rides at Stanley House. More and more owners were coming round to Lord Derby's far-sighted opinion . . . Carson was much, much more than just a handy lightweight.

In '73 Willie retained his championship. His rides increased from 829 to 883, and his winners from 132 to 163. Willie was certain that Parnell was the best he had ridden that year . . . and the unluckiest. As van Cutsem's assistant Mick Ryan stresses: 'They were a match made in heaven. Small but bighearted.'

Parnell opened his five-year-old career with an easy win in the Rouge Dragon Handicap at Ascot in April. To carry 9 stone 11 pounds to a 5 length win was no mean performance.

Willie was again in the saddle when the combination won the valuable Prix Jean Prat at Longchamp. They returned to France for the Grand Prix du Saint-Cloud and were fifth behind the Barry Hills-trained Rheingold, who in fact was never beaten on French soil.

After that came the King George VI and Queen Elizabeth Stakes at Ascot. The record books show that Parnell was fifth behind the flying filly Dahlia, but Carson will go to the grave convinced that he should have finished second that day.

Recalls Willie: 'Parnell was my unluckiest ride of the season. We were nearly knocked over on the bend into the straight. But for that we would have definitely been second. Rheingold, Our Mirage and Weaver's Hall were very lucky to finish in front of

Parnell.'

In 1979 when Carson coasted home on Troy in the King George VI, it was Paul Kelleway's Swiss Maid who nearly lost her footing on the final turn into the straight. Parnell received quite a bump from Dahlia as she flew through to the front. Parnell was just working his way forward when he got the bump.

Parnell was never seen with a chance for Carson behind Rheingold in the Arc de Triomphe. But he showed what a genuine horse he was when winning Newmarket's Jockey Club Cup. The stage was now set for Parnell to run his last race of the season.

Longchamp's marathon three-mile Prix Gladiateur was to be the race. Parnell, running brilliantly, finished first, but lost the prize in the stewards' room. Carson also picked up a four-day suspension for causing obstruction. Parnell hammered Forceful as he took up the running, and then hung left into the path of Lassalle.

Lassalle's trainer Richard Carver hates objecting, and he would have left the decision to the stewards. But the hooter was blown the moment the horses went over the line. Lassalle was promoted from second to be the winner. Parnell was relegated to third, which was severe punishment.

'Even though he had the race taken away from him, Parnell ran a cracking race,' said Willie.

Parnell did race as a six-year-old but was clearly over the top. By sheer determination he was placed in the Queen Alexandra Stakes at Royal Ascot and in the Goodwood Cup. He was retired to Ireland but was later exported to Brazil. Carson will always have happy memories of his association with Parnell, winner of fourteen races worth £118,612.

Willie's happiest moment in 1973 came in a lack-lustre mile race at Salisbury in August. He made all on the modest Tiercel to give veteran trainer Mrs Louie Dingwall her first winner of the season. There were tears in her eyes as Willie came back with his usual grin.

Silk Stocking's win in the Strensall Stakes at York in September gave Willie a great deal of satisfaction. 'The race was too short for her and they went too fast early on, leaving us well behind. But I managed to balance the filly and came through in the last yard,' said Willie.

Raceform noted: 'Silk Stocking, ridden and getting nowhere two furlongs from home, suddenly started to stay on in the softish ground. With the champion riding at his inspired best, Silk Stocking came from last place at the furlong marker to lead close home and win going away.'

Many times over the years Carson has been singled out for winning on horses which had no right to win. Willie was correct in assessing where his next challenge would come from for the jockey's title. In the autumn of 1973 Carson in his column in the *Sun* predicted: 'Pat Eddery will be my biggest rival in 1974. He's young, athletic and has a good style. He's also backed by Peter Walwyn's powerful stable.'

By now Carson was an international figure. Lester Piggott wasn't the only jockey with a much-stamped passport. Carson was in demand in Europe and most Sundays was seen jetting abroad.

For his final race of the season he was snapped up to ride Card King in the Washington International at Laurel Park. They finished fourth behind the fabulous Dahlia. Card King was Argentinian-bred and bought out of a Chantilly seller. Willie won the Grand Prix de Deauville on him.

Throughout the year the cry of, 'Come on Willie, my son,' echoed from every racecourse. He admitted: 'I'm only really happy for half an hour at a time. It only lasts until I get up on my next mount. I'm only happy when I'm riding winners. Each horse brings different problems. My life is a series of stepping stones spaced at thirty-minute intervals. When I don't win, I'm usually unhappy with myself or the horse. There aren't many in-between moods in this game.

'Pushing, that's my secret. Everything pushing – that's me. I just try to push them out to stretch them that little bit further, that's all.'

Carson was something of a reluctant champion. Always when pressed he stressed: 'Look, Lester is the real champion. We all know that. He's racing's brainbox. He works the form out better than men who have nothing else to do.

'It's now accepted that he can ring up any trainer and ask to ride his horse. All the owners want him, so he gets away with it.'

By 1973 there was not a single course among the thirty-seven flat tracks where Willie had not ridden a winner. When I visited him at Newmarket he told me: 'There is nothing finer than riding a winner. You feel that you have really achieved something.

'One day at Haydock I studied a photo-finish in which I had been involved with Lester. I could not tell from the photo which one was which, we were identical. We were using the whip in the same way and stretching the horses out.

'I thought that it was a great compliment we looked so alike. He's still the daddy of us all. Sometimes Lester has taken a hammering from the press over the way he has ridden but he just says, "Bloody fools – don't know what they are talking about."'

Jockeys are sensitive little creatures when it comes to press criticism. I heard one jockey tell a colleague: 'You wouldn't know the difference between a clothes-horse and a rocking-horse.' One forthright jump jockey told a Welsh colleague bluntly: 'The only good thing ever to come out of Wales was the M4.'

In the autumn of '73 Carson was approached by Barry Hills to be his first jockey. Rumours were spreading that van Cutsem, by now a sick man, was disheartened by labour problems in racing and was thinking of retirement.

But van Cutsem insisted: 'I am not retiring. I plan to have seventy horses in training in 1974.' Barry Hills was emerging as a brilliant young horse trainer, highlighted by his Arc de Triomphe win with Rheingold.

He offered Carson a hefty retainer – a bigger sum than he received at Stanley House. But by now Willie was actively involved in buying houses in Newmarket. Like his champion predecessor, Carson was not going to fritter away the big rewards of the Turf.

Carson turned down the Hills offer. They were to link up later. For Willie it was loyalty to van Cutsem, coupled with the dream of winning the Derby in those famous black Derby silks.

And the anonymous letter writer, who threatened to shoot Carson if van Cutsem did not get rid of him, was clearly not a man of his word.

8 The Dibidale jinx

Newbury's racecourse vet loaded his gun and slowly aimed at the head of a beautiful filly who lay sprawled on the ground. She had smashed her joint in so many pieces that it was like a box of matches.

'Stop it. You can't do that. For God's sake don't shoot her. She's too valuable as a filly,' screamed a crest-fallen Willie Carson and he saved the life – all too briefly – of the unluckiest filly ever not to win the Epsom Oaks.

Dibidale was her name. She could have been called Miss Tragedy. But like the Baskerville family there could have been an eerie curse which was to turn Lady Luck savagely against her.

Owner Nick Robinson named Dibidale after a beautiful stretch of water in the Outer Hebrides. Perhaps that was his first mistake as he relates: 'This loch is supposed to be haunted, and many of the locals refuse to go anywhere near it.

'The story goes that in days gone by one clan pushed a rival clan over the cliff and into the loch. When there's a full moon it is said that you can hear the haunted cry of the doomed clan come up from the depths of the dark waters.'

The fact that Dibidale was named after a loch was probably not in this brilliant filly's favour. I rate Dibidale as the unluckiest Flat-race loser I have ever seen, or am likely to.

And there are no prizes for guessing the unluckiest jump loser in my racing days . . . the Queen Mother's tragic Grand National hope Devon Loch.

If ever my overdraft extends to the limit of horse ownership I'd think twice about naming a horse after a loch.

And there's a further jinx which stretches back in Dibidale's family history. For it was on Dibidale's grandmother, Priddy Fair, that Joe Mercer's brother Manny was tragically killed after being thrown as he made his way to the start for the Red Deer Stakes at Ascot on 26 September 1959.

Dibidale was the final act of a bad-luck story, and Willie Carson's third in the 1974 Oaks will only survive the test of time because it was probably the finest exhibition of Flat-race horsemanship that we are ever likely to witness.

'The finest riding I've ever seen,' says likeable owner Robinson. 'Willie was in tears when he came back.'

It's racing history now how Dibidale finished third in the Oaks after Carson had ridden the filly for the last 2 furlongs bareback. The saddle slipped dramatically, shedding the weight cloth and the number cloth. Watching Willie actually try to ride a finish was unbelievable. Without being able to draw the weight Dibidale was disqualified and placed last.

According to Brian Taylor, who rode the last home Riboreen, Dibidale would 'have won by the length of the track. She'd have absolutely trotted up.'

Dibidale proved in the Irish Oaks that she was the rightful heroine at Epsom. But study every record book for a year and you won't find her name amongst the Epsom Oaks winners. Like Devon Loch, she goes down in Turf history best remembered for the race she didn't win.

Many owners who dabble in breeding never hit the jackpot. Some that do become pedigree and breeding experts overnight. Nick Robinson is frank enough to admit: 'Dibidale was a complete fluke.

'I owned Priddy Maid, who was by the luckless Priddy Fair, who was associated with the dreadful Manny Mercer incident. There was no staying up all night studying different pedigrees to find a suitable stallion for my mare.

'I was advised that the most important thing to remember when finding a stallion was to make sure that it was at a good stud where the foal would be properly born into the world. I was told that John Fenwick's stud at Six Mile Bottom near Newmarket had a marvellous stud groom. The only reason why Priddy Maid went to that particular stud was because of the groom – certainly not the stallion. That must be unusual.

'In fact I was disappointed when I learnt that the stud only had one stallion, Aggressor. He was terribly unfashionable and had not produced any outstanding stock, although, of course, he had defeated Petite Etoile in a controversial King George VI and Queen Elizabeth Stakes at Ascot.

'I then sold the mare to Robert Sangster carrying Dibidale but Joe French advised me that I simply had to buy back the foal. This I did for 3200 guineas.

'As a two-year-old she was a little backward. But Barry Hills had already taken a bit of a shine to her. He forecast that she would be a good filly in her own time.

'Willie Carson rode her first in a big maiden at Newmarket and finished sixth. I'll never forget the huge grin on his face when he came back. His face told the whole story, and Barry and I knew that we had something to look forward to.

'Willie's face tells all. He was delighted with her.

'Bernard van Cutsem claimed Willie when she had the second of her two races as a two-year-old. Brian Taylor rode her when she was backed down from 6–1 to 7–2 favourite for the Sandwich Maiden at Ascot on 13 October.

'Willie was again claimed for van Cutsem when Dibidale had her first race as a three-year-old. Barry thought that she was unbeatable, but there was not a lot of give in the ground and she did not want it firm.

'She opened at 5–4 but soon became the 8–13 favourite. Barry's confidence was clearly reflected in the market. Ironically, Willie Carson beat us by a head on Scientist. Trust him! You can never leave him out.

'In her next race, the Cheshire Oaks, we had Willie back in the saddle and Dibidale made all to win by 7 lengths from Mil's Bomb.

'We were really fancying her now for the Oaks but there was just the one fear about the ground being too firm.

'I was at Epsom the day before the Oaks and was really dejected. There wasn't a cloud in the sky and the sun was blazing down. The ground would have been all against the filly, and it had been rock hard for the Derby on the Wednesday.

'To try and buck me up, Barry Hills said that he and Willie

were flying to Haydock that night for an evening meeting. They invited me to go and I decided to, although I didn't have a toothbrush or any overnight gear with me.

'Just to add to our fears about the ground, from Gatwick all the way up to Haydock we never saw a single cloud.

'Barry won the first race at Haydock with Danum and Robert Sangster had a winner. I was still feeling pretty low and praying for a drop of rain, but it didn't seem very likely.

'We stayed with Robert for the night, and Barry and I agreed that although we had left Dibidale in the Oaks there was no possible way that we would run her unless the ground changed dramatically – and that seemed very unlikely.

'I'll never forget being woken up at six in the morning by the sound of a good thunderstorm. At seven o'clock we rang a friend in the south and heard that it was raining cats and dogs.

'Wonderful! Willie had always said that if the ground was soft she would not be beaten. That morning we rang Heathorn's who were quoting her at 10–1. Presumably they didn't think that she would run. But the firm were the only ones who were prepared to guarantee their prices up to noon on the day of the race.

'Every single owner in Barry's yard was on at 10–1. It would have been quite a severe reverse if Dibidale had won.

'It was still not as soft as we would have liked. In fact at the top of the hill I could see Willie losing his place. But you know Willie. He kept pushing along and suddenly the filly got the bit in her mouth and started to fly.

'At 3 furlongs out you could see that she was going to be a clear-cut winner. Then 2 out the dramatic moment happened. The saddle flew in the air and ended up under the filly.'

Robinson is certain that Dibidale jumped a path at the top of the hill and over-stretched herself. 'She was always a deep-hearted runner with little behind her,' he recalls sadly.

'Willie always said that if it had been any other filly she would have stopped dead in a stride. But she had a great temperament.'

Racegoers buzzed with excitement as they saw the saddle fly in the air and 10 pounds of lead in the weight cloth also flew in the faces of the following horses.

Epsom's masses then realized that Carson was not prepared to pull up. Providing an astonishing rodeo show, he continued to ride bareback.

Said a terribly disappointed Carson: 'Coming down the hill I knew first that something was wrong. The reins felt as if they were getting longer – but it was the saddle slipping backwards.

'I took a pull at Dibidale to keep the saddle in place but before the quarter-mile marker I knew that I had to get my feet out of the stirrups to stay aboard.

'The only time I thought that I would come off was when I was pulling up afterwards.'

Hills was quizzed by the stewards. He said: 'I don't think that anybody was to blame. She was saddled properly and checked again at the start. She tried to jump the path and was in effect trying to jump through her girths.'

Barry must curse the very existence of the unique, undulating twists and turns of Epsom. Irish jockey Liam Ward once told me: 'The bloody place wants blowing up. To run the world's greatest flat race round that gaff is a joke.' I suspect Hills feels the same.

He suffered the agony of seeing Ernie Johnson outgunned by Lester Piggott (Roberto), and his Rheingold pipped by inches in the 1972 Derby. Then came the luckless Dibidale's brave attempt when she finished third but the owner didn't receive a penny prize money.

But worse was to follow. In 1977 Durtal looked to have the Oaks at her mercy but threw Piggott in the pre-parade and never even took part in the race, for which she was a red-hot favourite. Then in the 1978 Derby Willie Shoemaker was pipped on Barry's Hawaiian Sound in a photo-finish by Shirley Heights after making all but the final yard of the running.

Hills's Epsom luck is nil. Little wonder he puffs at his giant cigars and admits: 'It doesn't seem to be my lucky track.' Too true!

The Epsom Oaks was won by Louis Freedman's Polygamy, who gave Pat Eddery his first Classic winner. While Carson's luck was out in 1974, Eddery was enjoying the luck of the Irish, although trainer Peter Walwyn did point out that he considered Polygamy an unlucky runner-up to the Queen's Highclere in the 1000 Guineas.

The scene was now set for a re-match with Polygamy. And in the Irish Guinness Oaks Dibidale proved conclusively that she was the real winner at Epsom.

It rained hard in Dublin and for once she had Lady Luck on her side. She also had another extra item of cargo . . . a safety device that made sure there was no repeat of the Epsom mishap. Dibidale from then on always raced in a breast-plate. It ran from below one side of the saddle, round the chest to the other side, and she resembled a hard-pulling Cheltenham Gold Cup favourite more than a silken lady speedster.

Before the Irish Oaks Carson told readers in the *Sun*: 'She'll gain her revenge – no problems. She has worked so well since Epsom that Barry is putting her in the same bracket as Rheingold. She could turn out to be not only the top three-year-old filly but the top three-year-old in Europe.'

Hills was certain that Dibidale would turn the Curragh re-match into a procession. He was right. Recalls Robinson: 'We were at a party the night before the race in Dublin, and Barry kept telling the home trainers, "Don't back Dibidale to win. Back her to win by 5 lengths."'

Hills was spot on. Dibidale won by 5 lengths from Gaily, with Polygamy a further 1½ lengths away in third. She proved conclusively that the slipped saddle cost her the race at Epsom. At the turn Dibidale was driven up into third place by Carson and, after storming into the lead 2 out, won unchallenged.

It was the display of a top-class filly and popular Michael O'Hehir, Ireland's answer to the familiar tones of Peter O'Sullevan, roared into his microphone: 'She's flying in . . . and there's no saddle slipping now.'

It was planned that Carson should now ride Dibidale in the Arc de Triomphe. Bookies made the Paris thriller a ladies' one-two-three by naming Allez France, Dahlia and Dibidale the first three in the betting. Robinson's filly would no doubt have got the softish going at Longchamp which she revelled in.

Said Willie after the Curragh walkover: 'I always knew that she had it in her. I tell you that she won't get beaten by the colts this season. The fillies have command at the moment and don't forget that we are entering the fillies' best time of the year. I believe Allez France will stand still but by the autumn Dibidale will have improved even more.'

The filly did her Arc prospects no harm in her next race, the Yorkshire Oaks. In a three-horse affair over the Knavesmire, Willie was forced to make the running. It was a slow gallop and I recall thinking that the 1–3 backers of the Irish Oaks winner were living very dangerously. It was only in the final 2 furlongs that Dibidale lengthened her stride and we saw her at full tilt. But Dibidale looked beaten when headed by Mil's Bomb. Running on again to display her great courage and stamina – plus Carson's driving – the favourite got up to win by a neck. In the Chester Oaks the margin had been 7 lengths between the two fillies. Perhaps the slow early pace had caused the clear-cut shortening of the winning margin. Or had Dibidale gone a little bit over the top?

We will never know. Clearly the flat-out gallop at Longchamp would have suited her better. But she suffered a hairline fracture of a pastern and was out of action for the rest of the season. In fact she didn't move out of her Lambourn box for two months. She missed a crack at the valuable Prix Vermeille en route for the Arc de Triomphe.

Early in 1975 Robert Sangster, who was just beginning to build up the breeding side of his world-wide racing empire, purchased a half-share in Dibidale, but she continued to race in Robinson's colours. Maybe Dibidale had been lucky to race in softish ground at the Curragh and to get up again to pip Mil's Bomb . . . but she never had any more luck in her life. Just the opposite.

In her first race as a four-year-old she beat only one in the Grand Prix du Saint-Cloud in June. And she was never seen with a chance in the epic Grundy *v.* Bustino clash in the King George VI and Queen Elizabeth Diamond Stakes of 1975 and was seventh of eleven.

Dibidale's farewell race was the Geoffrey Freer Stakes at Newbury on 16 August. She had hinted when finishing third in the Hardwicke Stakes behind Charlie Bubbles that there was still some sparkle left in her tank.

And indeed she was going well in the Geoffrey Freer until the final disaster of her luckless career happened. Recalls Robinson: 'All was going well until half-way. Then she suddenly gave a horrendous leap in the air and pulled herself up.

'It was then that the course vet thought there was no alternative but to shoot her. He was just about to fire his gun when Willie insisted that she should be given a chance to recover.

'The next race was put back slightly and she was put in a horse ambulance. Oddly enough it was her off foreleg pastern which had been injured this time and not the same one as before. The whole foot was put in a fibreglass case and she went back to Barry's.

'A week later she was in some distress and when the case was removed it was obvious that the whole foot had gone septic.' Says Hills, who even went as far as to praise Dibidale as the best horse he had ever trained: 'We tried for three weeks to save her. She had operations and anaesthetics and they knocked hell out of her. The only thing we could do was to put her down.'

Carson had given her a kindly reprieve. But it was only stalling the inevitable. There were more than forty different fractures in the one leg. What promised to be a great career at stud was ended by a vet. It was the kindest action.

On a slope of ground not far from Barry's house the remains of Dibidale are laid to rest. It's a peaceful spot and there is a tombstone to commemorate this outstanding South Bank filly.

If fortune had favoured the brave, Carson and Dibidale would have won the Epsom Oaks. Perhaps the author of destiny decided to pen an Oaks win for Carson in the Queen's purple-and-scarlet silks. Who knows? Maybe the ghosts of the legend from the Outer Hebrides laid their final curse on a filly named after the haunted loch.

There was a cruel jinx on the top fillies of that year. Besides the Dibidale tragedy, Mil's Bomb and Polygamy both died at stud.

And in America the four-year-old flying filly Ruffian shattered a pastern in an accident very similar to that of Dibidale. Not one of these lovely ladies was able to pass on their good looks and relentless gallops.

Willie will always be remembered for his fantastic bareback display. But he is saddled with the annoying memory of the

Epsom Oaks which was clearly his . . . only for it to slip away. Last word from owner Robinson. He told me: 'Barry was crazy about Dibidale. He loved her sweet, unflappable character.

'He said she was the only horse he knew that could be ridden to a cocktail party, tied up to a tree and after two hours' imbibing, she'd still be standing there waiting.'

9 'Prince William' abdicates

Willie Carson was made 2–1 favourite with Ladbrokes to clinch his third jockeys' championship in 1974. The layers had come to respect the all-action-pushing style of wee Willie and were not taking any chances. They knew better than most his whirlwind finishes.

Such was Carson's apparent domination of the jockeys' scene that bookies did not give any of the Scotsman's rivals a ghost of a chance of toppling him from the champion's pinnacle. The young Irishman, Pat Eddery, and Geoff Lewis were offered at 5–1 and Lester Piggott at 6–1. The rest of the country's top jockeys were out with the washing in the betting market.

Tony Murray, who had finished only eleven behind Carson in 1972, was one of many 25–1 shots. In racing the truest adage is that money talks – it usually yells actually. But on this occasion the bookies had it wrong, and those who tucked a Carson 2–1 on voucher into their wallets, looking forward to an autumn pay-out, were in for a shock.

In March Willie was at London's Dorchester Hotel to receive his Golden Spurs Award at the William Hill Organisation's annual lunch. After 142 winners in 1972 and 163 a year later, he seemed to have a great chance of landing a title hat-trick.

The late Sir Charles Clore made the presentation to Carson. Other award winners included Peter Walwyn, Fred Winter, Ron Barry and Arthur Budgett.

Carson, never lost for a quick giggle, amused guests at the lunch by spotting a piano at the Dorchester. He displayed his undoubted musical talents with a quick Liberace-style session at the piano.

In 1974 Carson was again retained by Lord Derby to ride his horses with Bernard van Cutsem. Other patrons in the Stanley House yard were now keen to use the champion – but not all of them. The Long Fella still lurked in the background. Willie had also struck up a good success rate with Barry Hills, the Lambourn trainer who saddled the luckless Dibidale. With these two influential trainers behind him, Willie looked to have the world at his feet.

But the season never really got going for him. Van Cutsem's tragic illness had started and his horses were never in top form. Besides the Dibidale incident, Willie had more than his share of bad luck. And for the first time since he hit the big time with the Lord Derby retainer he actually had more seconds than he had winners. In his entire fabulous career this has only happened three times . . . this shows a measure of the little man's consistency and power in the saddle.

In the season's first big race, the Lincoln, Willie teamed up with nearby Newmarket trainer Clive Brittain, a man who was to play a vital role in his career at a later stage.

At Doncaster Carson rode Olympic Casino for popular owner Harry Demitriou, who owns a plush casino of the same name in London's busy Queensway area. The moment Olympic Casino was linked with Carson his ante-post odds came tumbling down. Bookies always fear a big-name jockey on a good outsider. But this was an example of the odds being cut on reputation rather than straight cash support. Olympic Casino had won ten races in Greece but when he came to England the previous year he had failed to win in five trips from one mile to a mile and a half. He didn't appear to have the speed to win a Lincoln.

Yet he was reduced to 14–1, only to go wandering out to 28–1 on the day. He ran on to be fifth, but was never going to trouble Ryan Jarvis's Quizair.

Doncaster's three-day opener was a blank for Carson. Yet significantly Peter Walwyn unleashed two of his blue-bloods from Seven Barrows, Paper Palace and Tudor Rhythm, and they both won. Pat Eddery had made just the kind of start to the season Carson didn't want to see. The Walwyn–Eddery winners' factory were in business.

Two seconds at Leicester added to Carson's frustration and he had to wait until Mallane, trained by Gavin Hunter, won at Leicester on 26 March to open his account.

Bernard van Cutsem chose Leicester as the unlikely venue for Parnell's special tune-up for the season and Europe's top middle-distance races. Parnell had fourteen successes behind him. Van Cutsem was particularly keen on the leading French races suitable for his game trier.

Parnell, accompanied by Carson, looked impressive in his Budget Day work-out at Leicester after racing. In the one mile and a half post-race gallop he loved the soft ground and cruised clear of Varsity Match and Dynamic Dan, who were ridden by Jock Ferguson and Derek Morris.

I saw the gallop, and if you had told me that Parnell would never win another race in his life I would have advised you to take more tonic with the gin. But it's a sad fact that although he ran six races as a six-year-old he never got his head in front again.

Parnell and Carson were second in Longchamp's Prix de Barbeville on 7 April. They were beaten by Recupere, who went on to hand out a second beating in the Prix Jean Prat at Longchamp on 28 April. This was a race Parnell had won twice before. This time he was a sad fourth.

Recupere proved himself to be an outstanding stayer, for he went on to win the French equivalent of the Ascot Gold Cup, the Prix du Cadran at Longchamp on 26 May. This time Parnell finished fifth.

Parnell saved his best display for Royal Ascot, when he ran a good race to finish half a length behind King Levanstell in the Queen Alexandra Stakes. A third in Ayr's Tennent Trophy really proved the gutsy little horse was a light of other years. And defeat in the Goodwood Cup on 1 August persuaded van Cutsem to call it a day. Parnell, who won £118,612, was sent to stud in Ireland but was subsequently shipped off to Brazil.

At Goodwood van Cutsem claimed Carson for Parnell. Barry Hills was keen to have him for Proverb, a younger horse with better current form. But in his column in the *Sun* Carson insisted: 'I would always want to ride Parnell whether he wins or loses. He is my favourite horse.

'Parnell is such a gallant little fellow, although he hasn't had a good season. We are both in need of a win at the moment. Proverb won the Goodwood Cup last year and is a very kind horse. That's why I call him the gentle giant. I thought we put up his best display when second in the Ascot Gold Cup.'

Added Willie – then third in the table behind Eddery and Piggott – 'Lester is on the crest of a wave and it looks as though he will be champion. I can't put my finger on why things have not gone well for me. I've had more seconds than most people have had first courses!'

Piggott duly won on Proverb with Parnell third in his farewell race. Parnell joins High Top, Dunfermline, and Troy in Willie's top bracket.

Bookies refused to believe that Scotland's first-ever champion jockey would surrender his crown. At York in May Carson rode a treble on Lovelight, Kinglet and Avon Valley. Bookies than made Carson 7–4 on to win the title, although Eddery had shortened to 6–4. Said a relieved Willie: 'That's my first treble of the season. I reckon that my luck has changed at last.'

It followed his first Classic win of the season when he popped over to Germany to win their 1000 Guineas on Une Ami. Like Lester, virtually every Sunday saw Carson jetting to the Continent. Days off at the height of the season were as rare as triple dead-heats.

By Derby–Oaks time Carson's plans were not clear on the colts' race, although he was officially booked to ride the subsequently luckless Dibidale in the fillies' Classic.

Like Lester again there was tremendous speculation as to which colt Carson would ride. He had won for Dick Hern on Kinglet at York, and the pipe-smoking Major was impressed with his handling. For lightweights Hern made a mental note of Carson.

By mid May Hern engaged Carson to ride either Lady Beaverbrook's Bustino or Appleby Fair in the Derby. Stable jockey Joe Mercer was to have the first choice.

Appleby Fair then ruined his chances in the Predominate

Stakes at Goodwood when Mercer finished sixth on him. No Derby prospect this one.

It was Lady Beaverbrook's racing manager, Sir Gordon Richards, who advised Hern to have Carson standing by. Before the flop behind English Prince at Goodwood, the West Ilsley connections were sure that Mercer would go for Appleby Fair. But as Sir Gordon pointed out: 'Bustino has run in two Classic trials and won them both.' Mercer duly chose Bustino as his twenty-first Derby ride.

English Prince was yet another Walwyn–Eddery triumph. They simply couldn't stop having winners.

In 1974 racing was plagued by a classic Lester Piggott pre-Derby guessing game. The Long Fella had every other jockey quaking in his riding boots as the big day came nearer.

Finally it was announced that he would ride the Maurice Zilber-trained Mississippian – much to the anger of regular stable jockey Aussie Bill Pyers, whose language on the matter was nearly as colourful as his flame-red hair.

Then Zilber – later to boast that he could 'walk on water' – scratched Mississippian, and the journalists' and bookies' guessing game started all over again. Finally the maestro opted to ride Arthurian, an American-bred colt who only lost his maiden status at Newbury the previous month.

Arthurian started at 28–1, the longest-priced Derby ride for Piggott for many a day. There was no fairy-tale here and the duo finished twelfth.

Paul Cole, the talented Lambourn trainer, was quick to step in for Carson's services when Appleby Fair went out of the firing line. Cole gave Carson the leg up on Court Dancer, who finished ninth behind 50–1 runaway outsider Snow Knight.

Cole's yard was so badly hit by the virus that he did not imagine that he could have Court Dancer ready in time. Said Cole before the Derby: 'Court Dancer is one of the few Epsom runners who will definitely stay the trip. He won the Zetland Plate at Newmarket as a two-year-old and is by the 1957 St Leger winner Ballymoss.'

Said Willie: 'I don't know much about Court Dancer but his breeding certainly looks the part.'

Carson, set for his fifth Derby, told *Sun* readers, 'I usually take everything in my stride and don't suffer from nerves. But I do on Derby Day – all jockeys do.

'I have over 800 rides in a season but this is the only one which knots my stomach muscles. But I'll take a quick look round and it will be reassuring when I see other white faces straining to contain the tension and the anxiety.

'I suppose you could say that I'm a bit of an actor and this will be my stage. I'll be showing off Court Dancer to the greatest audience in the sports arena.'

Sadly Court Dancer never raised a quick-step and was always behind. Then three days later the Dibidale jinx struck, and a near-certain Oaks victory for Carson was snatched from him.

Lester Piggott's hunt for Derby rides did not altogether please other jockeys. Carson summed it up well: 'There is a fair possibility that someone will be jocked off in the Derby.

'He has the best record and that's why no one is safe when he goes hunting for a ride. It's a fact of life. The owners pay the bills and they are entitled to have who they want.

'I believe that there is more to life than just one race. But Lester is something special and we have just got to put up with it. I wouldn't like to see anything changed.

'When Lester got up on Roberto in the Derby and Rheingold in the Benson and Hedges, it's worth remembering that Bill Williamson and Yves Saint-Martin, who were jocked off, were not in fact the official stable jockeys.'

Royal Ascot started sensationally with the first three horses home in the opening Queen Anne Stakes all disqualified. Brook was upgraded from fourth to be awarded the race.

Bernard van Cutsem landed a colossal gamble with Old Lucky in the Royal Hunt Cup. Carson rode a perfect race and was not perturbed when the regal van Cutsem looked down in his special way and commented in the paddock: 'I've had a few shillings on here, Willie.' Carson was delighted by his win and commented: 'That makes up for last year when I got beaten by a head on Pontam. Old Lucky is a really honest and tough performer.'

This was a rare big-race success for van Cutsem, whose stable was not generally in good form. By the end of July Lester

Piggott had ninety-eight winners with Willie on eighty.

'I can't catch Piggott,' said a *News of the World* headline, and Willie told Robin Gray: 'I've no chance. It's too many winners to pull back. Especially when it's Lester you are up against.'

By September Carson – known by many Newmarket lads as Prince William – had abdicated his jockey's crown with two months of the season still to run.

He told the *Evening Standard*'s Chris Poole: 'I haven't a hope in hell of retaining the title. In fact, I gave up all thought of it ages ago.

'I haven't been getting so many good horses to ride. I have been trying just as hard as I did in the last two years, but it just hasn't been my year.

'If you look through the form book you'll see that I have ridden a tremendous number of seconds, while Lester and Pat Eddery have been riding winners. Bernard van Cutsem's horses have been a little disappointing and that has left me that vital twenty winners short.

'I suppose any jockey is only as good as the horses he rides. I'm disappointed at losing the title but it's not the end of the world.

'Lester will win the title, no doubt about it. He wants the championship back, don't let him kid you otherwise. Pat Eddery is running him close but I think his challenge will blow up in the next few weeks and he is likely to run short of good rides.

'I know Lester has commitments overseas but with such a wide choice of mounts he'll do it all right.'

I should add that Geoff Lewis once admitted to me: 'Jockeys are the worst judges in the world.' So it proved with Carson's tip of Piggott for the 1974 championship. Pat Eddery, the quiet, thoughtful Irishman, rode 148 winners from 749 rides to be champion. At twenty-two he was the youngest champion jockey for forty-nine years.

Piggott had 143 wins from 585 rides, Edward Hide 137 from 758 and Carson slipped back to fourth in the table with 129 from 908 rides. Significantly Piggott had a win percentage of 24.44, Eddery 19.76 and Carson 14.21.

It must be said that it was largely Peter Walwyn's tremendous ability to manage a team of 100-plus, added by his great enthusiasm, which turned the tide for Eddery. It was good revenge for Eddery to pip Piggott, as his father Jimmy Eddery had been unlucky to lose the 1957 Oaks on Silken Glider when only a fantastic display by Lester got the Queen's Carrozza up on the line and left her a very sore young lady.

Nothing went right for Carson. In the autumn he was booked by Barry Hills to ride Straight As A Die in the St Leger. Said Willie before: 'He is a bit one-paced, but if it rains he will have a chance. He must have it soft. If it's heavy he really will take some beating.'

Carson was injured when Piggott replaced him and finished third behind Bustino and English Prince in his last outing at York. Straight As A Die seemed certain to stay as he had finished only four lengths behind the crack French stayer, Sagaro, over 1 mile 7 furlongs, at Longchamp in June.

Alas, the rains never came and the Doncaster going was good ground. Carson forecast, 'I only have Bustino to beat,' and his forecast proved correct. Bustino and Joe Mercer gave Lady Beaverbrook a long-overdue Classic win, but Straight As A Die was a disappointing seventh and did one worse than Carson's ride for Barry Hills the previous year, Aureoletta, who had finished sixth.

A win on Ksar in the Premio del Sempione in Milan in September gave Willie a welcome boost. The £16,500 prize money meant a good cut for Carson and he admitted: 'Although I am not the champion I think I will have made more money this season. I've won quite a few big races and we get 7½ per cent of the prize money.'

Before the season ended, Carson took to hurdling – literally. At Nottingham he was forced to hurdle over fallen horses. After the crash Kipper Lynch and Willie Higgins were in hospital for three days.

Carson had won the Doncaster Cup on Proverb, and the scene was set for just one more big Flat race of the season, the Arc de Triomphe. Barry Hills was hopeful that Proverb would repeat the winning performance of his Rheingold the previous year.

Proverb had yet to race on the yielding ground usually in evidence at Longchamp in October. Sadly it was not his day, and Proverb was well back in fourteenth place as Yves Saint-Martin booted home the flying filly Allez France to be the undisputed Queen of Europe.

Carson had another disappointment for Barry Hills as he finished fourth on Celestial Dawn in the season's top sprint event, the Prix de l'Abbaye.

All in all it had been a disappointing season. But van Cutsem was quick to announce: 'The arrangement with Lord Derby continues. We will retain Willie in 1975.

'Of course, Willie has had an unlucky run recently but so does everybody else sooner or later. It never occurred to me to take on another rider.'

Carson said: 'As long as they want me I certainly would like to stay.'

Barry Hills had second claim on the energetic Scot in 1975. This meant many choice rides at Lambourn – plus the Stanley House horses.

Anybody who thought that we had seen the last of William Hunter Carson as champion should have been locked in a mental home. His genius, backed by a unique will-to-win, would see him back at the top again.

Hop-a-long Carson . . . Willie is pictured doing his John Wayne act with the six-shooters

Below left: Never gloss over Willie's achievements! In 1979 he proved a dab hand at Epsom before the Derby and his triumph on Troy. Smart work!

Below right: The Carson kids . . . Tony (left) and Neil pictured at Newmarket in 1978

Above left: The easiest Epsom Derby winner for half a century. Terrific Troy and Carson roar home by 7 lengths in 1979. Troy made the rest look like wooden horses

Left: Steady boy! Willie steers Troy back to the winner's enclosure at Epsom after a fabulous win in the 200th running of the Derby

Above: He's done it again! Troy has beaten his all-age rivals in the 1979 King George VI and Queen Elizabeth Diamond Stakes at Ascot. Willie explains the triumph to trainer Major Dick Hern, while stable lad David Gillespie shows his pleasure

Hats off to Her Majesty! Willie Carson in joyous mood after The Queen's Dunfermline had beaten Alleged in the 1978 St Leger. Obviously delighted, Lord Porchester looks on

10 'You can't beat a trier'

Thursday 1 May 1975 was the ugliest day in the history of the Turf. It saw the charge of the light brigade at Newmarket, where after 300 years of racing we saw the unprecedented sight of 100 striking stable lads staging a human wall of defiance across the Rowley Mile.

'Is this the end of life as we know it?' inquired the racing correspondent of *The Times* to a press colleague, as he gazed in sheer disbelief at the battle of Newmarket.

And at the height of the melée Willie Carson was sensationally dragged from his mount by a group of striking lads. It was a sad day in racing's history and one which will not be forgotten quickly by those present.

The drama centred on a wages demand by the Newmarket stable-lads. Over the years the little men had been clearly underpaid. The lads were regarded as a very unimportant part of the industry and they had no official voice to air their claim.

Often these men tended and cared for animals worth a small fortune. Yet one heard of stories like the millionaire owner who marched into Henry Cecil's yard just before Christmas one year and handed over a ten shilling note for the lads, who were looking after his string of horses worth thousands.

The lads clearly had a right for an increase in wages. And when they joined the Transport and General Workers Union the whole picture of a wages negotiation changed dramatically. Early in the century a lad hopefully asking for a little bit more money would probably have received a belt round the ear by the trainer, on his way to a pre-dinner cocktail after evening stables. But with the full might of the TGWU behind the lads, their strength greatly increased.

Sam Horncastle, the union's regional organizer, became a thorn in the side of the trainers. With racing's hierarchy and establishment trainers at headquarters, he was fast proving as unpopular as Dan Dawson had been in the first half of the nineteenth century.

The Newmarket Trainers' Federation was led by John Winter, brother of jumping ace Fred Winter. He took over Highfield stables when his father died in 1965.

John Winter is a charming man and he was rather unfortunate to be the man in the hot seat when the lads decided that they deserved a substantial wage increase.

The day of the 1000 Guineas was when it all happened. The Jockey Club allowed the striking lads to picket on their private property on the racecourse.

The stable lads had hoped that fellow union members operating the photo-finish camera and other course facilities would strike in sympathy. But the men worked as normal, and the photo-finish was used to check when Nocturnal Spree, trained in Ireland by Stuart Murless, short-headed the 1000 Guineas. Carson was unplaced on Bernard van Cutsem's filly Monaco Melody.

The Guineas was the fourth race on the card but the incident to recall came before the second race, the Brethy Handicap.

Even before that racing pickets had tried to stop punters, owners and trainers entering the course. With the exception of four coach drivers – also members of the TGWU – who agreed not to cross the picket line, the move failed.

There was the unpleasant spectacle of lads thumping and banging on the sides of the horse boxes as they tried to make their way to the course stables.

Realizing that they could not halt the meeting, the strikers ran on to the course and staged a sit-down on the track, which delayed the start of the first race until police persuaded them to move.

The battle of Newmarket occurred as Willie Carson and others cantered down to the start of the 6 furlong race. Willie was dragged from Pericet and beaten by his own whip. Other riders were chased across the track by the lads waving banners.

Horses turned and shied until one group led by Lester Piggott rode their mounts through the strikers at speed, both to break up the line and also to prevent themselves being pulled off.

Said Carson: 'A crowd of lads surrounded me as I rode up towards the starting gate. Some were for me . . . and some against me.

'My whip was grabbed from me and I was pulled from my horse. I was hit over the back of my left leg with my own whip. It certainly hurt me and I lost my temper. It was stinging and I was mad.

'I saw the other horses had got through the boys' picket line and that I was left on my own. I had run into the back of Greville Starkey's horse Import and had come to a standstill.

'I never hit anybody. I thought I would go back and get a bit of help. Some people were already coming. I just gave them a wave to come and help.

'Before the race I had sympathy for the stable lads – I was one myself once. But people are not going to sympathize with the lads when they do things like this. All my sympathy has evaporated after this.'

It was Carson's wave to the crowd which prompted many racegoers to mount the barrier and storm down the track towards the lads. By sheer weight of numbers they were able to push and manhandle the lads off the track, and the meeting resumed over half an hour late.

Bruce Raymond was on Tingo – and he stayed on. He said: 'We were circling around and couldn't get by. Then Lester Piggott said: "Let's charge," so we got through.'

John Winter alleged that the strikers were being supported by professional left-wing militants. He said: 'The strong-arm boys have now moved in.

'This is nothing to do with trainers *v.* stable lads any more.'

The action of the racegoers to remove the strikers was, according to former Jockey Club senior steward, General Sir Randle Feilden, 'spontaneous'. The general was a far-sighted racing supremo, but proved that he was a little out of touch with modern-day life when asked about the introduction of a minimum wage for lads. He gave the classic reply: 'I would not dream of asking Jeremy [Tree] how much he is paying his butler.'

That almost rates with the answer I received from Lord Leverhulme, another former Jockey Club senior steward, when I suggested that many owners would be financially driven out of racing if the minimum training fee was introduced. 'Oh, they can always own greyhounds,' came the somewhat shattering reply. The interview was taped at the Jockey Club's insistence and when the 'they can own greyhounds' line was produced the head of the Racing Information Bureau, who was present, nearly had a fit.

I was asked not to use that quote as it was 'not quite meant as it sounded'. As they had the answer on tape I felt quite entitled to report the conversation.

The racegoers, dressed in military-style overcoats, trilby hats, cavalry twill trousers and suede boots, won the day. A few well-aimed shooting sticks, swinging binoculars and the occasional well-heeled boot won the battle of Newmarket.

Thankfully, the stable lads' strike was finally settled. Memories of the incident still rankle with many senior Newmarket trainers. Mention of Mr Horncastle is the proverbial red rag to a bull.

For John Winter it was not a happy experience. Four years later he told me: 'It was a very harrowing time. But I like to think that I didn't make any bad friends.

'In the end the lads got a £5 a week increase to bring them up to £37. This was for a 40 hour week but they had to do 3½ hours overtime every other weekend.

'It was one of those things that I was chairman of the Federation at the time. I must admit that it did nearly put me out of business. I had a terrible outbreak of the virus at the time and was also just starting BRIC. Added to all that I had to spend so much time on the strike.

'The incidents on the racecourse were a shock. The Jockey Club allowed the lads to picket on their property, but the lads went a step further and sat down across the course.

'The strike did have its good results. Previously Newmarket had to do all the wage bargaining and then the rest of the country followed suit. Now it is done annually on a national basis all over the country and this has taken the pressure away from Newmarket.'

But Winter still thinks that many 'outsiders' were called in to support the lads. He claims: 'The strike was not really about money at all. It was the manipulation of a small town.'

Tony Murray, who rode The Blues in the controversial race, did report: 'If some of those chaps down there are stable-lads, then I'd love to see the horses they ride. They must be as big as houses.'

Bernard van Cutsem's sad death in 1975 produced a turning-point in Willie Carson's career. The year of 1975 was not an altogether happy one for Carson, and for the second successive year he had to surrender the jockey's crown to Pat Eddery.

The young Irishman had the full might of Peter Walwyn behind him, highlighted by the Lambourn duo taking the Derby with Grundy. At the end of the season Eddery had booted home 164 winners from 816 rides. Carson rode two more winners than the previous season and his total of 131 from 846 rides took him into second place behind Eddery.

Lovers of statistics would quickly point out that this gave Eddery an average of 20.10 per cent wins, while Carson was on 15.49 per cent.

Yet it was a totally muddling year for Willie. Obviously van Cutsem's Stanley House stables were bound to be affected by their outstanding trainer's illness, although assistant Mick Ryan did a fine job. Usually van Cutsem turned out over sixty winners but in his last year the figure dropped to twenty-two.

Carson had struck up a good relationship with Barry Hills and was riding most of the Lambourn trainer's horses. In 1975 Barry saddled eighty-one winners and was only fourth behind Peter Walwyn, Henry Cecil and Ryan Price in the money-winning list. Clearly Hills, with Rheingold's Arc victory in 1973 already behind him, was very much an up-and-coming trainer. With the death of van Cutsem it seemed obvious that Carson would make an ideal stable jockey for the talented master of South Bank.

But not for the first time Carson was to be 'jocked off' in favour of Lester Piggott, and such was Willie's anger that he decided that he could not ride for a stable where this was likely to happen.

Although Willie had been champion jockey on two occasions the menace of owners wanting the Long Fella still haunted him. Carson was greatly to be admired. He had sufficient faith in his own ability to part with Hills, who it must be said was not responsible for the amazing switch of jockeys.

Solitary Hail, an American-bred colt by Hail to Reason, caused the shock split. Yet Carson and Robert Sangster's colt could hardly have started their racecourse relationship on a happier note.

In Ascot's Glanville Stakes on 25 July Solitary Hail was backed down to 5–1 on the basis of good, strong work at home and duly won in Carson's usual urging style by 1½ lengths.

In his next race Solitary Hail was beaten into second . . . but when you consider that the hero of that particular day turned out to be no less a colt than Wollow there must have been ample excuse.

Doncaster's Laurent Perrier Champagne Stakes saw Franco Dettori swoop by the ideally placed Carson to go on and win by 1½ lengths. If Carson could have been blamed for that defeat then I must have been watching the wrong race. Wollow was never beaten as a two-year-old in four races and went on to win the 2000 Guineas in great style.

Yet when Solitary Hail ran in the Observer Gold Cup at Doncaster on 25 October . . . yes, you've guessed . . . Lester Piggott was given the ride.

Before the Observer, Hills and Carson decided that the end was in sight. Their good trainer–jockey relationship was on the rocks, spoilt by the latest Piggott 'jockeying-off' situation.

Hills said: 'I see Solitary Hail as a good Derby prospect for next season – either at Epsom or the Curragh. I discount his defeat by Wollow.

'He did not race properly that day. He ran like a rusty knife but the Doncaster Mile will suit him down to the ground.

'Robert Sangster asked me to engage Lester if he was available – and that's exactly what happened.

'Willie has never done anything wrong on the colt and I loathe having to do it. But to say we have had a row is a load of rubbish.'

Ironically, while Solitary Hail was a dismal flop in tenth (beating only Jack Hardy's debut-making High Prince), Carson finished seventh on Coin of Gold.

Solitary Hail was backed down to 7–4 favourite. Noted Raceform, 'He never held out the slightest hopes. Behind and ridden early on.'

This was the last time Solitary Hail was ever seen on an English course, as he never raced as a three-year-old. But he will go down in Turf history as the colt who forced Carson to take an ambitious and brave action which was to lead him in yet another direction in his career.

The day after Solitary Hail's sad performance – and Willie would have been hardly human if he had not noted the result with one of his impish grins – Carson gained some compensation.

Riding Roan Star, the only two-year-old in the field, he won the Group One £60,000 Prix de la Forêt at Longchamp – the last big French race of the season. It must have been a sweet victory for the deposed Carson.

This was a happier French raid by Carson that the one to Deauville in August when he was suspended for four days after his mount Tarik had finished third in the Prix Maurice de Gheest, only to be disqualified for bumping.

Before his split with Barry Hills, Carson was the usual rider of a really remarkable filly called Duboff, who won nine of her eleven races in 1975.

She ended her brilliant campaign with a fine win in the Sun Chariot Stakes at Newmarket on 4 October, when she beat such good female rivals as Mil's Bomb and Roussalka.

Her only defeats both came outside England. In the Irish Guinness Oaks she finished tenth (ridden by Ernie Johnson), and in the Prix de la Nonette at Longchamp on 7 September she was last with Carson on top. Still she was a very successful young lady. She cost just 9400 guineas and opened her winning career in a lack-lustre Windsor maiden.

Carson, who had scored his fifth consecutive century when winning on Great Brother in the Arlington Stakes at Newbury on 20 September, had already aroused the interest of one leading patron just before the Solitary Hail split up.

Hills was sorry to lose Carson's services. He said: 'Of course, I love Willie riding for me. Who wouldn't?'

Later in this biography you will learn how the Vernons Pools supremo, Robert Sangster, a few years hence attempted to sign up Willie Carson. Perhaps with the memory of the Observer Gold Cup fiasco still burning painfully in his mind, Willie declined a substantially increased retainer. And this led to the American wonder boy, Steve 'The Kid' Cauthen, coming to England in 1979.

With the death of van Cutsem and the split with Barry Hills, Willie Carson said good-bye to two huge equine armies, one encamped at Newmarket and the other at Lambourn. Many lesser men would have stayed with Hills and been only too glad of the job. But with Willie it was a point of principle.

But if he was worried where his next retainer was coming from, he didn't have many sleepless nights. With his never-give-in tactics now famous, the telephone was sure to ring.

And when the phone did ring the voice at the other end of the line was one of the nicest guys the racing game has ever known . . . Clive Brittain.

Carson was snapped up by Brittain, or rather by his leading patron Captain Marcos Lemos. He owned Great Brother, the colt who had given Carson his fifth century on the trot.

The Greek shipping company director had been a superb supporter of English racing. Yet after his first venture into ownership it's a wonder that he ever bid for a second horse in his life.

In the sixties he staggered the sales ring when he paid 27,000 guineas for Grecian Sea, who was far and away the highest-priced yearling of that year. Trained by Ron Smyth, he was unfortunate enough to break a leg, he never even saw a racecourse and had to be put down.

Most men would have cursed their luck and vowed never to nod for a single horse ever again. Not so Marcos. The man with the wonderful war record was not to be disheartened.

He splashed out vast sums – and still does. In 1973 his Cavo Doro, ridden by Lester Piggott, was second in the Derby behind Morston. His other outstanding horse was Petingo, who won the Gimcrack, Middle Park and Sussex Stakes, when trained by Sam Armstrong. Carson was at St Gatien when Petingo proved himself an outstanding miler. But for the brilliance of Sir Ivor he would surely have been a 2000 Guineas winner.

Ironically Petingo was to prove himself a good sire, and in 1979 Carson was to team up in breathtaking fashion with his most famous offspring . . . terrific Troy.

Captain Lemos, who has also ploughed much money into various charities including the one for stable lads, owns the Warren Hill and Ashley Heath studs at Newmarket and bought the Carlburg Stables from David Robinson, where his present trainer Clive Brittain now operates.

Recalls Marcos: 'We already had a kind of second claim on Willie after Bernard van Cutsem. He was always one of the tip-top jockeys. I liked him very much. He was always very pleasant. He will always smile, but deep down he is very professional.

'Some horses are difficult to ride, but Willie always gets that little bit extra out of them. He's so clever in that he always seems to work out the actual character of a horse and then adjust his tactics to suit the animal.'

The linking of a Greek shipping millionaire and a one-time Sir Noel Murless apprentice is as unlikely as you can imagine. But Captain Lemos and Clive Brittain form one of racing's most charming owner-trainer partnerships. Despite hefty outlays at the sales rings they have not achieved shattering success, but they are a popular pair and nobody in the game could have denied them their moment of Classic glory in 1978 when Julio Mariner finally justified his promise in the St Leger.

Brittain was with Sir Noel Murless for many years and rose to the position of travelling head lad. He talks lovingly of Crepello – 'the best I ever saw' – and other star inmates of the superbly trained Warren Place stables. With such a good pedigree in racing it was obvious that one day Clive would turn to training.

In 1972 he started with thirty-two horses at Pegasus House, Newmarket. By 1977 he had moved to Carlburg and had 108 horses. The head lad had certainly emerged as one of our biggest-string trainers – backed by the desire of Marcos Lemos to win the big prizes.

It's history now that at the Derby meeting in 1976 the dumb-founded racing world learned that Joe Mercer had been replaced by Willie Carson as first jockey to Dick Hern after over twenty years' loyal service to the patrons, who included the Queen. Thus Carson only had one season with Brittain as his official jockey . . . and it's a fact that Brittain will regret and Lemos will rue for many a year to come.

Marcos Lemos explains: 'It wasn't the way Willie decided to leave us. It was the way the whole wretched business was announced. I first heard the news on television. I still maintain that I should have been told first.

'I think that Joe wanted to clear the air and that's why it came out. But Willie must have been keeping quiet for a long time. Still, it doesn't do any good to be annoyed. Willie has ridden for us several times since.'

Clive Brittain, always a smiling and immaculate figure on the racecourses, remains one of Willie's greatest admirers. He confides: 'If the offer to replace Joe Mercer had come a year later I think that we would have enjoyed enough success ourselves for Willie to want to stay.'

Quiz Brittain about the best rides he has seen from the wee Scot and he quickly grins: 'For me or against me, do you mean?' During their year together, Clive selects Carson's display on Patris when he dead-heated with another of his horses, Radetzky, only to be disqualified and placed third.

Says Brittain: 'Willie lost it in the stewards' room but I'll never forget what he did on the course. Yves Saint-Martin on the French horse Earth Spirit was actually hanging into Willie and he did miracles to get a dead-heat.

'Since then the really memorable ones have all been against me. At Doncaster in September 1979 I saddled Marcello for the Sancton Stakes. With fifty yards to go Eddie Hide was 3–1 on to win for me. There wasn't a chance that he could possibly be beaten.

'Then from nowhere comes Willie on Dick Hern's Water Mill and pips us by a neck. I couldn't believe it. It was sheer genius.

'Earlier in the year at Haydock I had another reason to curse the little so-and-so. A furlong out in the Fred Archer Handicap in April it seemed that Edward had the race absolutely sewn up on Rheinford. It was just a matter of them coming home. Then Willie started to pick up Ryan Price's Speed Bonnie Boat and they came and beat us by half a length. That was another brilliant performance of jockeyship.

'I am certain that Willie is getting better all the time. We have always known that he has terrific strength in his small frame. But now he is beginning to understand the different types of horses. That is bound to be acquired only by experience. I really believe that we still haven't seen the best of him yet.

'I was lucky to get him for that short spell. He never would have left Bernard van Cutsem. My first yard at Pegasus used to back on to his former home and, although an apprentice rode my first winner, Willie was a big help in the early days and rode many of the winners.

'The announcement of the move to Dick Hern was very unfortunate. It was rather sprung on Willie. The Captain was upset at the time. He never says one thing and means another. But he has ridden for us since and any disagreement is now over.

'When I was with Sir Noel Murless in the early days, I used to think that Sir Gordon Richards was a terrific jockey. There's no doubt that in his era he was out on his own. Nobody could touch him.

'But when Lester Piggott came along I think that he raised the pace and other jockeys simply had to follow. I think the standard of riding is higher than it's ever been – and it's far straighter too.

'Sir Gordon was peerless but today we have Lester, Willie and also fine riders like Joe Mercer, Pat Eddery and Greville Starkey.

'Many people think that Willie has a happy-go-lucky personality. That's true, but there is also a very serious side to him. He never gets off a horse without offering an opinion. He is by far his worst critic and I have often heard him say on dismounting, "Sorry. It was my fault."

'He never took much interest in the entries – that never

bothered him. But he had definite views on every horse he rode. Often he used to tell me that we were running horses way out of their class – too ambitious – and then he'd ride his heart out to prove himself wrong. It was remarkable.

'I recall one day at Brighton I ran a horse and really fancied him. But despite Willie trying like mad, the horse finished so far back you couldn't see him.

'Willie came back and grinned as usual. He said, "What are you going to do with this one? He'll never win a race."

'Then three weeks later at Beverley he rode the race of his life and was only beaten a short head on this same old plater.

'His only problem in the early seventies was that he was inclined to get shut in on occasions. He was always so cool and used to keep his head while others around him were up to all sorts of tricks. Sometimes he'd admit that he had been shut in.

'You know what he is like. He won't give an inch to anybody. Others had to go through him or had to go round him. Sure, we lost one or two in the stewards' room. But you can't beat a trier.

'He's the greatest last-minute man I know. You have to get up five minutes early to beat him. He's a brinkman.

'I remember one day I ran a horse called Pipeline at Ponte-fract. We really fancied him and had gone for a good touch. Willie had been riding in Germany, and I was worried when I heard that his plane had been delayed and he was due in late at London Airport.

'I began to think that I'd have to get another jockey. I worked it out that there was no possible way he could drive from Heathrow and get to Pontefract in time.

'I daren't tell you how long it took him. But just as I was about to get a replacement I heard that familiar little shuffling trot up to the clerk of the scales.

'As usual he was laughing and pushing people out of the way. God, he's a determined little fellow. That hectic drive from the airport didn't seem to unnerve him. The horse duly won.'

It seems amazing now, but Captain Marcos Lemos actually sacked Carson with three weeks of his contract to go in 1976. The owner was still irate about the mid-season announcement of the switch to Dick Hern.

Carson rode Derringo in the Highflyer Stakes at Newmarket on Cesarewitch day, 16 October. Captain Lemos did not think that Willie had made sufficient effort. They had in fact finished sixth. Said Willie after the shock ending of the contract: 'Me, of all people. I'm usually accused of trying too hard.' It was the sad end of the partnership.

Richard Fox had already been lined up as the new stable jockey. Said Brittain at the time: 'I am very sorry about all this. The Captain feels that Richard might as well get used to some of the horses that he will be riding next year.

'Willie will continue to partner the rest of my horses and I hope he will continue to ride for me next year when he is available.'

Fox, from the Frenchie Nicholson riding academy, was really thrown in at the deep end with little experience, and the move did not work. He also finally got the thumbs down from the Captain, and Edward Hide was lured from the north by what was supposed to be the biggest retainer in racing.

But that partnership also ended after a short spell. At the big Goodwood meeting in 1979 Brittain announced that the ex-cock o' the north was returning to Yorkshire to join Bill Watts. Hide also nearly suffered the indignity of being relieved of his job with only a few weeks to run like Carson.

He had the Follifoot Handicap in his grasp on Petronisi and was fourth, lengths clear, coming into the final furlong. Suddenly Hide dropped his hands, and Yamadori just failed by a short head to take advantage of the lapse.

Said an angry Lemos: 'That would have been it if he had been beaten here.' Star apprentice Paul Bradwell became the stable's big riding hope.

Willie again lost the title in 1975, although John Oaksey in the *Sunday Telegraph* had advised his readers before the start of the season: 'It seems to me that much the most attractive price on offer is the 3–1 against Carson. In the last two seasons I can honestly say that I cannot remember seeing him lose a race which he should have won.'

Title and Classic glory did not go Willie's way but in June he went to Redcar for five rides . . . and won on all of them. Gan on Geordie (100–30), Claudio Nicolai (11–2), Holdforth Boy

(15–8), Noble Game (3–1) and Breathing Exercise (6–5) made it a memorable day for Willie's army of supporters. Four of the winners were trained by Denys Smith.

Rose Bowl, the unluckiest filly never to win the 1000 Guineas, took the Queen Elizabeth II Stakes, and then Willie scored another notable win when the filly beat the one-time Queen of Europe, Allez France, in the Champion Stakes.

This was when Daniel Wildenstein – so incensed when his beloved Yves Saint-Martin was 'jocked off' by Lester Piggott on Rheingold at York – adopted different tactics and publicly slammed his jockey for arriving late on the scene.

Willie was having a monster clean-up in the Queen Elizabeth II. Rose Bowl gave him wins in 1975 and 1976. Then he booted home the next two winners, Trusted (1977) and Homing (1978), before finishing sixth on Bolide, behind Kris, in 1979 to end his four-timer.

Willie was seventh on Royal Manacle in the 1975 Derby – his fifth ride in the race. A year later he partnered Tierra Fuego for Clive Brittain but was unplaced. Said Brittain then: 'Willie has never ridden better in his life. Willie started me off by riding so many of my early winners, and now I'd love to make him champion again. Half of his winners have been for me in this our last season together.

'I'll run three in the Derby and I don't know which is best. But I wouldn't dream of engaging jockeys until I have finalized my plans. I believe in only firm bookings.'

Willie scored his second Great Met. win on True Lad in 1976 (he had won on Lyford Cay, also for Bill Swainson, in 1972).

11 'Did he smile when he got off?'

'Are you going to tell them, Dick, or am I . . . ?' With these ten words the fate of Joe Mercer, first jockey to the West Ilsley stable for over twenty years, was sealed.

In the press-room at Epsom at the 1976 Derby meeting Lord Porchester, The Queen's racing manager, and West Ilsley trainer Major Dick Hern announced the shattering news that veteran Mercer was fired and Willie Carson appointed in his place.

If the press had been informed that Lord Wigg had been elected to the Jockey Club they would not have been more surprised.

First as stable jockey to Jack Colling and then from 1962 with Dick Hern, Mercer had become part of the West Ilsley success story. Initially Joe had been apprenticed near Wantage in 1947 and rode his first winner on Eldoret at Bath in 1950.

At West Ilsley he soon became associated with horses running in the colours of the stable's owners – the Astor family. In 1953 in typical classic style, which he copied mainly from his late brother Manny, Joe booted home Lord Astor's Ambiguity to win the Oaks.

Hornbeam (a fine stayer), Indian Twilight, Military Law, Master of Arts, Alcimedes and Paul Jones were just a few of his early big-race winners.

By the early sixties he was associated with Escort, Never Say and River Chanter. In 1964 Joe enjoyed his best season with 106 winners – notably on Lord Astor's Grey of Falloden in the Cesarewitch and the Doncaster Cup.

A year later he rode the same number of winners, including

the St Leger on Jakie Astor's Provoke and the Irish St Leger ten days later on Lord Astor's Craighouse.

As Dick Hern, a great horseman in every sense, emerged as one of the best trainers in the land, his jockey Mercer rode some outstanding races. Few people could have guessed that the storm clouds were gathering for pipe-smoking Joe.

1971 saw the climax of Mercer's West Ilsley connections when he won the 2000 Guineas on Brigadier Gerard. In all the Brigadier won seventeen of his eighteen races. His one defeat came in the Benson and Hedges Gold Cup at York when the American jockey Brailo Baeza made all on Roberto to flaw the odds-on Brigadier.

One connection of the Brigadier was annoyed enough to comment rather unsportingly: 'Roberto must have been stung by a bee – or something.' Later experience of this race rather proved that it comes too soon for horses who, like the Brigadier, had a hard race in the King George VI and Queen Elizabeth Stakes.

In 1974 Mercer won the 1000 Guineas on The Queen's Highclere and the St Leger on Lady Beaverbrook's Bustino. Roche Noire was his 2000th winner at Brighton on 2 September 1975.

Joe not only won the English 1000 Guineas, but amid great excitement rode the royal colours to victory on the same wonderful filly in the Prix de Diane at Chantilly when Her Majesty was present. The French went mad and cheered heartily.

But within two years Mercer was sacked as first jockey at West Ilsley. And for the first time two very remarkable men were to emerge as the new force behind Willie Carson's career.

'Perhaps they are going for greater experience,' a clearly distressed Mercer told pressmen at Epsom. It was his one hint of bitterness that, at the age of forty-two and in his prime, he was being replaced by a man eight years younger.

The 'they' Mercer was referring to were the men now to retain Carson . . . Sir Michael Sobell and his son-in-law, Sir Arnold Weinstock.

Sir Michael, born of Jewish parents in Austria in 1892, came to England when he was twelve and became a brilliant industrialist. He was knighted for his tremendous work for charities.

Sir Arnold, who married Sir Michael's daughter Netta in 1949, is the son of a Polish tailor. From a humble start in north London's Stoke Newington he became the top industrialist in Britain and from 1962 he has headed the vast business empire of the mighty G E C organization.

G E C employ over 175,000 personnel and are the largest private employers in Britain. But it was the taking on of just one all-action man in racing, Willie Carson, which sparked off much discussion and undoubted bad feeling.

Indeed, who would ever have thought that it would be two outstanding businessmen, with minds as sharp as razors, who would one day decide who should ride the Monarch's horses? It seems unlikely but that is exactly what happened.

The grace and beauty of classically bred horses galloping across the Berkshire Downs seems a million miles removed from the hustle and bustle of London's Park Lane. But in the heart of London Sir Arnold Weinstock not only masterminds G E C and its huge business outlets, from light bulbs to TV sets, but now pulls all the vital strings concerning the West Ilsley stables.

An essentially private man, Sir Arnold shuns publicity like the plague. One critic once accused him by saying, 'All he cares about is earning a fair return on shareholders' capital.'

Another conversation in the City between senior officials went: 'How do you think the Government is doing?' Back came the reply: 'I'll tell you the infallible indicator – is Sir Arnold Weinstock investing any of his cash yet?'

Such is the regard for Weinstock the businessman that the City talks of the Weinstock Indicator. By shrewd, and no doubt sometimes ruthless, business deals, G E C at one stage in 1979 had accumulated £730 million. As one City journalist commented: 'Now that Sir Arnold has acquired such a high, and deserved, reputation as Britain's most proficient industrialist, where he goes lesser mortals try to follow.'

Just five days before Troy's gallant third in the Arc de Triomphe I gained a rare interview with Sir Arnold at his London offices. He looks every inch the highly successful businessman, who gained a degree in statistics at London University and went on to work at one stage in the Admiralty.

Within minutes of a glimpse into his high-powered world, the telephone calls reveal the ace businessman . . . and the other big love of his life, horse racing.

Puffing at a cigar he tells one caller: 'Wall Street will surely go against us.' Then it's, 'Hello Gordon – who do you say that filly is by?'

Then his brain is clearly working even harder as he says: 'Yes, Dick. Did you work Troy? With Town and Country? Did Willie smile when he got off?'

This is the world of Sir Arnold talking to his racing manager, Sir Gordon Richards, and his trainer Dick Hern. And for the first time he reveals the fascinating background of how he and his father-in-law came to be so powerful as racehorse owners that not even The Queen could decide who dons the purple and scarlet silks at West Ilsley.

Sir Arnold told me: 'My father was born in Poland at the end of the last century. Sadly, he died when I was only five. From a very early age I started taking an interest in horses. I think the first course I ever went to was Kempton, but I can vividly recall watching Gordon booting home the winners at Ally Pally.

'I met my wife at a charity ball at the Dorchester in 1949.' This is significant, as Sir Michael Sobell's work for charity is quite remarkable. And it's worth noting that the GEC shareholders' report to the end of March 1979 revealed a profit of £214.6 millions, while 'charitable donations by the company, including donations to universities, amounted to £193,000. No contributions for political purposes were made.'

Sir Arnold then reveals the day he got the shock of his life. 'Sir Michael came to me and said that he had decided to buy a racehorse. He had shown no interest in horses whatsoever, so I was quite amazed. He didn't know the first thing about the game.

'My brothers and I had rather got the bug. I remember we had a nice little tickle at ante-post on the Cesarewitch before the war. Then I remember the first Derby I really got involved in was in 1948, when Nimbus won. Horses like Anchor's Away and Halloween were among my favourites just after the war.

'I was always keen on racing, but when my father-in-law told me he was thinking of getting a horse I could think of nothing less likely. It was in 1957 and we went in with our usual proportions . . . two-thirds to him and one-third to me. All the horses run in our pale blue colours with yellow and white cap.

'Sir Michael decided that he should buy a horse called London Cry, and sent him to Sir Gordon who was by then training. I dashed to the form book and saw that he had won the Craven Stakes as a three-year-old and had been sixteenth in the Derby. Since then he had run in blinkers and his form had got steadily worse.

'We did away with the blinkers and he seemed to improve at home. Our first run as owners saw London Cry beaten a short head at Salisbury.

'In 1958 I laid out £200 on London Cry for the Cambridgeshire and he duly won at 22–1. He was ridden by Scobie Breasley, as were most of our early horses.

'Ante-post betting is virtually my only interest in betting. My business is not really playing the stock market either. I have certainly no interest in casinos, and I've never been inside a betting shop in my life.

'London Cry carried 9 stone 5 pounds, which was then the highest weight carried of the century. We also had a good chaser in Flame Gun, whom Fred Winter once described as the best two-miler he had ever ridden.

'I was a great Scobie Breasley fan. He rode for us for ten years and I was very sad when he retired. He was a real craftsman with such a fine touch. He had a lovely finesse and his style was so beautiful.

'After London Cry's win we were all becoming addicted. We paid only 3500 guineas for him, and before the Cambridgeshire he had won five other races, including the Chesterfield Cup at Goodwood.

'We then decided to go into racing in a slightly bigger way. Our business interests were expanding very rapidly but racing was a good hobby.

'I remember Gordon saying that we should buy the best horses. I said that I didn't realize there was a way of sorting out the best horses just like that. He said, "The best horses will cost

10,000 guineas and not 1000 guineas.'' I thought it was all a dicey business, and there was no guarantee that any horse costing 10,000 guineas would be any better than the cheaper ones.

'By 1960 we had bought some expensive horses but things had not turned out very well. After the death of the Hon. Dorothy Paget we were approached by the executors to buy the Ballymacoll Stud Farm in County Meath in Eire. We paid £250,000 for the stud, which at the time seemed a big sum.

'Buying at the sales had not been totally satisfactory and we decided that it would be best to breed our own horses. When we took over the stud there were horses everywhere . . . about 200 of them. We had to do some pruning out.

'In 1960 Sunny Cove, who had been bred at Ballymacoll, won the Park Hill Stakes and the Newmarket Oaks. She proved the start of our own breeding lines and was later the dam of Crucible, by Crepello, who won races in England but achieved better success as a gelding in France when trained by John Cunnington junior. He won over £30,000 in all.

'Reform, Sallust, Sun Prince and Homeric were all bred at our stud and were good winners. When Sir Gordon's lease ended at Fordingbridge, he decided to retire and Dick Hern became our trainer.

'I knew Jakie Astor well and I said to him that if he ever decided to sell West Ilsley that we would be interested. That's how we came to buy the stables.

'We soon learnt quite a lot about the breeding side. It was pointless to think that you could breed high-class animals all the time. The object was to breed the best possible racehorses. We had an absence of speed in our matings and bought shares in Prince Gift and Whistler.

'In 1967 Dart Board was third in the Derby behind Royal Palace. I never really get terribly excited before a race. I try to think that every race is a contest which you obviously want your horse to win. But I do agree that it's silly to think that the Derby is the same as a maiden race at Chepstow. There's a difference in degree, but not a difference in kind.

'My son, Simon, was at Winchester about this time, and by 1965 he had become an expert in the breeding side of racing. He knew all the blood lines and it was his ideas which were responsible for the horses we bred like Sun Prince, Admetus and Homeric. At Winchester he was able to go down to Fording-bridge, and he soon struck up a good relationship with Gordon Richards.

'Simon is a banker now but he was at Oxford University. While he was there he was able to spend a couple of mornings on the gallops at West Ilsley. He decides all the matings now and his knowledge has been extremely helpful. Five years ago Sir Michael gave me his share of the stud in Ireland and Simon became a partner.'

Sir Arnold adopts a serious attitude when he speaks of the only controversial aspect of his highly successful spell of owner-ship with Sir Michael, which was highlighted by Willie Carson's dual Derby wins on Troy . . . the Joe Mercer exit from West Ilsley.

He told me: 'Quite frankly, I don't have to explain myself. We own the majority of the horses in the yard – and indeed the yard itself. It's got to be the owners' choice who rides for them.

'But I will admit that it was a painful thing, and in some quarters we have never been quite forgiven. The wound has never quite healed.

'I was trying to be rational. Even in business, if somebody presents a good reason why my opinion is wrong I will straight away give way.

'Some people wrote some stupid things at the time about the incident. We were accused of being the only owners in the yard who held the opinion that a change was needed. We weren't.

'I said nothing at the time. The advantages of taking on Willie Carson were far more important than the little things which made us think that Joe Mercer should be replaced.

'It suited us so well to get Willie. He can ride for us for ten to twenty years. It is a long-term arrangement. I will say that sometimes you hit it off with people and sometimes you don't. With Willie I get on much better than I did with Joe.

'When Bernard van Cutsem died we decided to approach Willie. When he told Sir Gordon and Dick Hern he was keen, we let Joe know a full year before that we intended changing our stable jockey. He had lots of notice.

'It was just that it was round Derby time that he pressed us to know for sure whether he would keep his retainer for the following year. I admit that the news was let out at a bad time and not in the right way.

'I was keen that Mercer should end with us while he still had enough of his riding career left to go on and get another good retainer. It has worked out with his move to Henry Cecil and he has done marvellously well.

'I don't know of a better jockey than Willie Carson. Lester Piggott was and still is something special. I'd go so far as to say that he's not normal.

'Willie is first class. His courage is tremendous. He simply loves the horses, and he laughs and smiles a lot. Of course, in his job there are moments when he comes under stress.

'For all his laughing and joking he is deadly serious under it all.

'Actually we seldom speak. I remember the Saturday before the 1979 Derby Troy worked on the Downs at Epsom. Willie got off and said simply, "Went all right." But he was grinning broadly so I knew that he was happy. There wasn't anything else to discuss.

'If he does have something really important to say, he tells Dick Hern and then he tells me. There is no point telling a jockey like Willie how to ride a race. If he doesn't know, nobody does. I notice that some other trainers nag their jockeys. I can never see the point in that.'

Sir Arnold rarely enjoys the City articles about his success at the head of such a powerful company. He says with typical honesty: 'I accept that in my position I will attract publicity. But that does not mean that I enjoy it.

'Articles about GEC tend to personalize the entire success down to one man. It's wrong. As it was said about Wellington and the Battle of Waterloo . . . it wasn't only him. There were a large number of cooks who helped in the victory.'

One item of publicity must have angered Sir Arnold back in 1972. He was put up as a member of the exclusive 209-year-old London club, Brook's, by Lord Aldington (the former deputy chairman of the Tory party) and banker Charles Villiers but was 'black-balled'.

Reflects Sir Arnold: 'I have no idea what particular form of nastiness prevented me from joining. Anyway I was not desperately keen. I just went there for dinner and said what a nice place it was. I was more annoyed for my friends who put me up and others who were members. They felt so strongly about the incident that they resigned.'

Thankfully the racing industry – and its 'in-crowd' – have not shunned the Sobell–Weinstock duo like they did the one-time super-owner David Robinson, who rather like Sir Michael made his fortune from the early days of radio manufacturing.

It remains one of the biggest slurs on the racing industry, and the so-called hierarchy of Newmarket, that Robinson was not encouraged to take an even fuller part in the sport. True, he pioneered the way for the blanket-coverage ownership of Robert Sangster and others. But his reception from racing's establishment was nothing short of insanity. Nothing demonstrated the stupidity of officialdom more than when his plan for a swimming pool and other facilities for stable lads in Newmarket was rejected.

David Robinson duly ended his successful love affair with the Turf and piled a fortune into a new college at near-by Cambridge University. Millions which could have benefited the racing industry were lost because of the folly of a few men – one of whom in the immortal words of a certain trainer based not a million miles from Worthing 'would be hard pushed to train rabbits to make love'. Pardon the abridged version!

Sir Michael Sobell was knighted for his philanthropy. Over the years millions have been donated to the care of the elderly and sick, to orphans, and medical research into such pressing problems as cancer, via the Sobell Trust.

Sir Arnold shares his father-in-law's concern for the less fortunate. Later you will learn how Troy, guided by his faithful partner Willie Carson, provided extra millions for charity by his deeds on the racecourses. Few people who watched this brilliant pair could have dreamt that so much help to the sick and infirm was being created by their galloping exploits.

Sir Arnold Weinstock acknowledges that the Mercer incident still leaves a scar on the West Ilsley horizon. But any man who pays the piper calls the tune. In this case not only did these two immensely successful men own the majority of the horses, they actually owned the premises on which they were trained . . . a similar situation to Bruce Hobbs' at Newmarket's Palace House stables, which has seen jockey comings and goings in recent years.

Racing is a curious sport. Owners who are successful can never guarantee that their victories will be admired by the masses. Success and popularity are vastly different commodities. Sir Michael and Sir Arnold may still not be top of the popularity poll, despite their staggering donations to charity.

Discussing his racing life Sir Arnold reveals: 'It's doing it all together which is the real dividend. Discussing plans with Gordon and Dick. Chatting to Willie after a race. That's the most enjoyable aspect.

'You know, at the end of 1978 Robert Sangster offered Willie Carson a fortune to be his jockey. Willie turned him down. Money isn't everything to him.'

Money was not the most important factor when Troy's future was being discussed in the autumn of 1979. Reveals Sir Arnold: 'From August onwards the Americans were on to us. One agent was prepared to give me an open cheque.

'We were offered much, much more to let him go to stud in America. But Sir Michael and I were both very keen that he should remain in England.

'Towards the end of Troy's career Sir Michael and I agreed that much of the prize money he had won should be converted to the Sobell Trust and be made available for charity.

'Frankly, there was no obligation for us not to send him to America. But I asked The Queen's racing manager, Lord Porchester, to try to get a syndicate together in Britain and we had a very good response – more than I expected.'

Sir Arnold is full of praise for Dick Hern's training methods and the riding performances of Willie Carson. 'Dick has a great feeling for horses,' he says.

Unlike most people in horse racing Sir Arnold is not superstitious. 'All that business about walking under ladders is not for me,' he says. 'I don't give it a second thought.

'But actually there is just one superstition that I have to do with racing. I never say that a horse looks well before a race. I never say that one of our horses looks the pick of the paddock, and I hate to hear anybody else comment in this way.'

Troy's unforgettable Derby victories came after twenty-one years in racing for Sir Michael Sobell and his son-in-law.

Sir Arnold, whose brilliant business brain has secured him a position at the apex of British industry with a salary three times the Prime Minister's annual income, gives a rare glimpse of his racing Weinstock Indicator by saying: 'Quite often Willie gets off and criticizes himself.

'It comes simply from a desire to excel. He's striving to be better . . . and that comes from a basic humility and wanting to reach an exalted position.'

12 'You don't need Joe – here I am!'

Willie Carson made a dream start to his career as first jockey to Major Dick Hern. Racing's vultures, those 'experts' who pack every grandstand, were ready to crucify him if he did not make a success of the job popular Joe Mercer had lost so sensationally.

Because of the insistence of two shrewd businessmen, Sir Michael Sobell and Sir Arnold Weinstock, even The Queen was left with little option but to use the strong-armed Scot. But Willie wasted no time in proving that he was capable of donning with distinction the famous purple silks with gold braid and scarlet sleeves.

In a fairy-tale start to Her Majesty's Jubilee Year, Carson won the Oaks and the St Leger on Dunfermline. This success all went back to the autumn of 1956 when The Queen visited Doncaster yearling sales prior to watching her High Veldt run into fifth behind Cambremer in the St Leger.

There must be something about the Doncaster sales ring. Ginger McCain's legendary nod at 5000 guineas secured the then unknown Red Rum, and it was at the same venue that The Queen obtained the pedigree which led to her dual Classic heroine Dunfermline.

Lord Porchester, the modern-day racing manager of The Queen who also has reason to bless the Doncaster sales, takes up the story. 'The Queen was keen to buy one particular filly. We walked round to the box and saw her.

'As we walked back The Queen noticed another little chestnut filly. She immediately looked the filly up in the catalogue and said to her party, "I want to buy her. That's going to be my little bit of fun." She was a Luminary filly and came from the same line as The Queen's Royal Hunt Cup winner, Choir Boy.

'The filly did not come up until the final morning of the sales and was then bought on The Queen's behalf for 1150 guineas. She was the bargain buy of the sales.

'Named Stroma by Her Majesty, she was placed three times but it was at stud that she created greater glory. She was to become the dam of The Queen's Eclipse Stakes winner Canisbay and the second dam of Dunfermline.'

Towards the end of the sixties The Queen instructed Lord Porchester to form a committee to look into her stud and racing interests. In 1969 Lord Porchester became the racing manager to this very remarkable racehorse owner.

'I'm an enthusiast. So is The Queen. And Willie Carson certainly is too,' said Henry George Reginald Molyeux Herbert Porchester, son of Lord Carnarvon, at the end of the 1979 Flat season, relaxing at his Berkshire home.

His enthusiasm was fired by the arrival the very same day at his near-by Highclere stud of dual Derby hero Troy. 'Isn't it exciting?' he beamed.

'It's all done in this tiny study,' said Lord Porchester. On one wall is a chart showing the pattern races – he is chairman of the Race Planning Committee – while another shows his connection with local government with a plan of proposed motorways.

Milford is Lord Porchester's home. Just a few miles from Newbury, it has a beautiful setting with a tree-lined drive down to the house situated in front of a magnificent lake.

It is here that so many of the decisions regarding the breeding and race plans of Her Majesty's racing team have been decided by her successful and ever-enthusiastic racing manager.

In his lounge a striking photograph of The Queen is autographed 'Elizabeth R'. Another photograph signed simply 'Dickie' recalls the recent horror so close to our shores.

But pride of place goes to a painting of Tamerlane. 'Ah yes,' said Lord Porchester with a happy smile. 'It was at Doncaster sales again. I had decided to buy this colt with a little bit of money I had won by backing another horse.

'I was standing with Paddy Prendergast and unfortunately I discovered that he was after the same colt too. Paddy told me, "I will have more money than you, Henry." I thought that there was no earthly chance that I would get the colt.

'The bidding was between us and we were standing together. When it got to 5000 guineas I rushed round to the other side of the sales ring and bid 5250 guineas. The auctioneer said, "New bidder," and Paddy Prendergast turned and walked away.

'When he heard that the colt had been knocked down to me he was very angry. The fresh bidder bit had fooled him. I told him, "I knew I was pretty hot but I never thought that I would out-hot you."'

Tamerlane was Lord Porchester's most successful buy. He recalls: 'Rae Johnstone told me that he didn't think that the colt would stay a yard over six furlongs, so it was lovely when Billy Nevitt beat him at Stockton in impressive style.

'Rae Johnstone came back and said, "I was wrong." Of course, we fancied him like hell for the 2000 Guineas, and my trainer Jack Clayton had him in perfect shape.

'Sure, he was very unlucky. Scobie Breasley had won both the 2000 and 1000 Guineas before, but he had not had many rides at Newmarket. He made his run at the bottom of the dip rather than at the top, and he was pipped by Our Babu by a neck in 1955.

'We now had to think about the Derby. Charlie Smirke offered to ride him and was very keen. Jack Clayton thought that it might be cruel on a little horse and so I struck him out of the Derby.

'Captain Elsey had bet £1 each-way on Tamerlane for the Derby and was furious when he was scratched. "You only have one chance in a lifetime to run a colt in the Derby and you must be mad not to take it," he told me.

'Owing to a rail strike there was no Royal Ascot in June that year. We thought that he was a good thing for the St James's Palace Stakes, but instead he had to go to Birmingham to win his next race. Then Royal Ascot was reinstituted, and he won the St James's Palace a month late.

'He also beat Retrial, who went on to win the Cambridge-shire. No, Tamerlane was a good horse, and had been third in the Middle Park as a two-year-old.'

Thinking no doubt of the Highclere arrival of Troy for a syndication of £7.5 million, Lord Porchester sighed: 'And do you know what I got for Tamerlane? £25,000! Just think what a horse like him would be worth today.'

Returning to The Queen's clever buy of Stroma, Lord Porchester commented: 'Her Majesty always knows the breeding lines backwards. Perhaps, like me, she knows the breeding best a little bit back. Neither of us are quite so well up on the American lines, which now have such an important part in modern-day racing.

'Stroma was given an easy race by Harry Carr in Epsom's Acorn Stakes, but she did not act on the course and was never quite the same.

'The first yearling I arranged to buy for Her Majesty when I became racing manager was Blue Danube.

'Actually I never thought that I would have time to do the job of racing manager. I had a very busy public life and was chairman of Hampshire County Council at the time.

'In those early days we had great fun with a number of horses. It was wonderful when The Queen was at Doncaster to see Charlton win the William Hill Gold Trophy. Example was a great mare and won the Prix Jean de Chaudenay, Prix Royal-lieu and the Park Hill.

'St Patrick's Blue won the Timeform Gold Cup and Albany was a remarkable mare. We would get her in foal, and she would get much stronger and go and win good races. She was fifth in the Oaks and was later to breed Card Player and English Harbour.

'When Sir Cecil Boyd-Rochford retired in 1968 we decided to split the Royal horses between Ian Balding at near-by Kingsclere and Dick Hern at West Ilsley, which is also very handy. Later we also sent horses to William Hastings-Bass at Newmarket.

'In previous times one owner with twenty horses would probably have had them all with the one trainer. Now it's best to have them divided, if only to avoid the diseases which are now so much a part of racing.'

Lord Porchester's face lit up when he recalled Highclere, The Queen's filly who won the 1000 Guineas and the French Oaks, the Prix de Diane at Chantilly.

Photographs from Chantilly show Lord Porchester on his feet, cheering Highclere and Joe Mercer over the line. I wonder if he could ever have guessed that within four years Joe Mercer would have been replaced by Willie Carson.

Said Lord Porchester: 'Before the 1000 Guineas I had a long chat with Joe Mercer. The filly had worked well but he told me, "You're mad if you think she will win the 1000. She wants over 1¼ miles now and has no earthly chance in the Classic."

'I recalled that Queen's Hussar had worn blinkers when he did his best work. In her last race as a two-year-old, when she struggled to win at Newbury when odds-on, Highclere had seemed to stare about her.

'I suggested before the Guineas that Highclere would be suited by blinkers. There was a great horror when I made the suggestion, but The Queen finally agreed.

'Highclere duly won the 1000 Guineas by a short head from Polygamy. After the race I was asked by pressmen where I thought Highclere would run next. I said, "Why don't you ask the owner?" The Queen said immediately: "I think the filly would be better suited to the Prix Diane than Epsom." How right she was!'

'The greatest day of our lives' was how Joe Mercer summed up Highclere's win in France. Twenty-two runners went to post, but Mercer scored by 2 lengths and sent the French crowd wild with delight.

Said Lord Porchester: 'The crowd went mad. It was a memorable day.' Scenes like it had never been seen at Chantilly before, as the crowd yelled: '*La Reine*,' and greeted the most popular of winners.

Later as the Herns and the Mercers were approaching Shoreham, Sussex, in their light aeroplane, a message was relayed from the Queen's Flight that The Queen hoped that they would all come to dinner at Windsor Castle.

The successful party of trainer and jockey thought that the message was a hoax but they duly diverted to Heathrow, dashed to Windsor Castle and made up a memorable celebration dinner with The Queen, Prince Philip, the Queen Mother, Princess Anne, Lord Mountbatten, Lord and Lady Porchester, and The Queen's stud manager, Michael Oswald.

Recalls Lord Porchester: 'It was a marvellous occasion. I remember Joe arriving all sweaty after a hectic journey and us smartening him up in the gents.'

In the middle of the dining-room table was the gold trophy presented to The Queen by Marcel Boussac at Chantilly only a few hours before.

Lord Porchester, who has stood next to The Queen and shared with her the moments of Turf glory and disappointment, thinks that Highclere then ran the race of her life to be second to Dahlia in the King George VI and Queen Elizabeth Stakes.

'That was an even better performance to my mind than winning the Guineas or in France,' he says. 'But she rather deceived us in the Benson and Hedges when she had actually gone over the top and it was a big mistake ever to run her in the Arc de Triomphe.'

The scene was now set for the exit of Mercer and the arrival at West Ilsley of chirpy Carson. What was the Royal reaction?

Reveals His Lordship: 'It was a very, very sad occasion. Joe is a marvellous chap and I am devoted to him. I am also a great Carson fan and equally devoted to him as well.

'The Queen was very distressed that Joe was going. But she said that the owners had a majority of the horses and also owned the yard, and there was nothing that we could do.

'We discussed the possibility of having two jockeys. Joe might still have been able to ride the Royal horses. But that would not have worked. You can't have two number one jockeys in one stable.

'Willie was a wonderful replacement. We could not have asked for a better rider. I had always thought that one day he might be our man. Sir Arnold was looking to the long-term situation.'

At the time of the 1976 Derby when the announcement was made, there was one of the seemingly never-ending financial crises in Britain. Lord Porchester warned Sir Arnold that when the announcement was made, 'The pound will be knocked off the front page of the *Evening Standard*.' True enough, the London evening paper announced in its lead story, 'Royal jockey sacked.' Lord Porchester was correct in that the West Ilsley barons underestimated the popularity and public feeling for Joe Mercer.

Thanks to the blood-lines stretching back to little Stroma, when Carson took over the Dick Hern job in 1977 he was introduced to a powerful filly with Classic hopes – Dunfermline.

Mercer had been third on the daughter of Derby winner Royal Palace as a two-year-old in her debut at Sandown. Then in the race after Crow had won the St Leger, Dunfermline and Joe were second in the May Hill Stakes at Doncaster. Then in the Argos Star Fillies Mile at Ascot she had to be content with second again.

Says Lord Porchester: 'I loved her the moment I saw her. She was always a marvellous mover. She was a great walker, although back at the knee.

'Dick always liked her very much. Actually I nearly had a fit when she made her debut at Sandown. It was so firm and dusty that I was scared stiff that she would do herself a terrible injury, especially with her fine action.

'She never travelled well and sweated up a little on the trip to Doncaster. There was just the slightest suggestion that she had not put it all in. It's always there with certain horses.

'At Ascot with her maiden allowance we thought that she would win. Again we thought that she might have slightly hung fire. Blinkers were talked about, but Joe Mercer insisted to us that it was not needed and she was just a bit green.

'I think that Lester Piggott commented that she was after all by a St Paddy mare and was really a three-year-old type being trained for a two-year-old.

'There was that tiny question mark hanging over her about whether she was 100 per cent genuine. The Queen thought the same, but she was not really a fully furnished filly at that stage.

'Unfortunately horses do not seem quite as honest these days as they were before.'

Carson quickly settled in at West Ilsley. He was inclined to think that two other fillies, Circlet and Lady Beaverbrook's

Topbird, were just as promising as Dunfermline. Ironically, Circlet never won as a three-year-old, and Topbird had only two wins from eleven outings.

Carson had his first public ride on Dunfermline in the Pretty Polly Stakes at Newmarket on 27 April. Relates Lord Porchester: 'She had worked marvellously at home, and we thought that she had definitely gone the right way from two- to three-years-old.

'She won easily by four lengths and the decision was now whether to run her in the Oaks. The big question was whether she would act. She had such a good action that there were real fears as to whether Epsom would be her downfall.

'The Queen was in the middle of her Jubilee Year and terribly busy. I don't think that she believed that Dunfermline would win the Epsom Oaks. Her Majesty was very worried about the filly acting on the unusual course, and I think she also feared that Dunfermline might simply not be good enough.

'It was touch and go whether she ran. Finally The Queen said, "Yes," but it took a great deal of thought. Prince Andrew was returning from Canada that day, and The Queen decided not to go to Epsom. She watched the race on television at Windsor Castle.'

Willie Carson's ninth Derby ride had proved an agonizing experience. Lester Piggott had won the Chester Vase by 5 lengths on Lord Leverhulme's Hot Grove. He was asked to ride the colt in the Derby but opted instead for The Minstrel, who had been beaten in both the English and Irish 2000 Guineas.

It seemed an odd choice, but Piggott kept his faith in The Minstrel, although some will say that he worked hard to get the ride on the Aga Khan's 9–4 favourite, Blushing Groom, who finished third.

Carson took the ride on Hot Grove. He had a super ride down Tattenham Hill and kicked off in front 3 furlongs out. Carson seemed to have the Derby in the bag. Piggott loomed up on The Minstrel 3 furlongs out, and it soon became a battle between the two.

Very close to home, Piggott conjured up that little extra from Robert Sangster's colt and he sneaked home by a neck in a memorable finish. It was tough luck for Carson, who rode a blinder, and the brave Hot Grove.

Two years later, when Carson won on Troy, he was asked how it felt to be out in front. In gleeful mood he beamed: 'Great. But all the time I was thinking of when the Long Fella came and did me before.'

Three days later the scene was set for the Jubilee Year Oaks. But there was drama galore before the race. Carson was involved in a car accident on his way to the course, and Dick Hern and Lord Porchester stood worriedly at the weighing-room door to see whether their pilot would make it in time.

Says Lord Porchester: 'I was very worried. I actually went as far as engaging Joe Mercer to stand by in case Willie did not make it in time. That would have been ironical.

'Suddenly we heard that Carson laugh and he burst in, saying, "You don't need, Joe. Here I am."'

The second drama happened when the likely favourite Durtal was involved in a pre-race accident with Lester on board and had to be scratched. Dunfermline actually sweated up in the paddock, and at Tattenham Corner still had plenty to do. That was where the Carson push was seen to work wonders and she came bursting through to hold off Freeze The Secret by three-quarters of a length.

Carson told Lord Porchester: 'She won it by guts. Terrific. I was just a shade worried about her staying but she did it nicely.'

Would Durtal have won? Not for Lord Porchester who told me: 'There must have been doubts about her staying. And anyway she seemed to be in a muck sweat a long time before the race.'

Immediately after Dunfermline's victory Lord Porchester dashed to the nearest phone and telephoned Windsor Castle. The Royal party already knew the result and were naturally thrilled.

The Queen's racing manager was quick to snap up odds of 33–1 offered about Dunfermline for the St Leger. It was about this time that Vincent O'Brien's super colt Alleged was getting into winning ways and would obviously be a Leger hot-pot.

But Dunfermline didn't seem to advertise her chances well

in the Yorkshire Oaks on 16 August. Starting at 11–10 favourite, Dunfermline was never able to strike a blow and was third behind Peter Walwyn's Busaca.

In the previous race, the valuable Benson and Hedges Gold Cup, Carson rode a peach of a race on Lady Beaverbrook's Relkino and trounced 11–8 favourite Artaius by four lengths. Yet again the Benson and Hedges had seen the warm favourite go up in smoke.

'No gallop. The pace was not nearly strong enough,' recalls Lord Porchester of Dunfermline's shock York defeat. The rules of racing state that every horse must run on merit and be put in a race with a view to doing its very best.

Pacemakers, legal in France, are a controversial subject in Britain. But according to Lord Porchester, chairman of the Pattern Race Committee, they should certainly be allowed to take their place.

'It is vital that races are run at a genuine pace. There is nothing worse than 1¼ mile horses being allowed to win 1½ mile races which have turned into a sprint for the last part of the race. I've never made any secret that after York we used a pacemaker for Dunfermline. The animals concerned were always doing their best and we were certain that it was going to be a good gallop.

'Even after the York defeat I did not think that my Leger bet at 33–1 was wasted. One day at Sandown I was a little bit gloomy. Sheilah Hern told me not to be downcast. 'If you had seen Dunfermline gallop at West Ilsley you would not be unhappy,' she said.

Yet again The Queen was to miss Dunfermline scoring a Classic win. This time she was at Balmoral, where Mr James Callaghan was a guest.

Alleged was 7–4 on favourite for the St Leger on 10 September. This time Dick Hern ran Gregarious as a pacemaker with Alan Bond on board. The 50–1 outsider set off like a scalded cat, making certain that the race was run at a good gallop. This did not really suit Alleged, who had cantered away with the Great Voltiguer and was unbeaten. He was the hottest Leger favourite since Nijinsky beat the Queen's Charlton seven years earlier.

Says Carson: 'Alleged seemed unbeatable. But Dunfermline's last gallop at home went so well that I thought I must have a chance.'

Gregarious led into the straight, but then Alleged was forced to hit the front. Carson was always in the leading bunch, and he waited behind Lester for his moment to pounce.

Just below the distance Dunfermline headed Alleged, and these two outstanding horses, and jockeys, battled for supremacy. Proving herself to be a great battler, Dunfermline, driven by an inspired Carson, won by 1½ lengths. Alleged was never beaten before or afterwards, and that included two fabulous Arc de Triomphe victories.

Recalls Lord Porchester: 'I'll never forget the noise of the huge crowd. I've never heard such a din on a racecourse. It was wonderful to hear the crowd cheer home the two horses. It was a great shame that The Queen was not there to see it.

'Our plan with Gregarious worked out just right for Dunfermline. The pace was ideal. There was a stewards' inquiry but Willie always said that he would keep the race.'

Dick Hern looks back: 'If it had not been for the terrific gallop set by Gregarious we might well have been beaten.'

Lord Porchester slams his table to emphasize his point when he says: 'To my dying day I will insist that Dunfermline should have been first or second in the Arc de Triomphe. Perhaps from the stands it is impossible to criticize Willie.

'Gregarious had been injured, and we did not bother to have a pacemaker. It was a mistake. We thought that some of the other leading French fancies were sure to have a pacemaker to make it a good gallop.

'Instead Lester seemed to dictate the pace throughout. When he made his move there was that split-second when Willie could have gone with him. There was no gallop, and Willie knew that after Doncaster he was certain to stay on the better.

'Dunfermline lost a plate during the race and that didn't help. She was boxed in a little but was flying at the finish, and I think that she would have run Alleged much closer if Willie had gone for home that split-second sooner. We knew that she had superior stamina.'

I might add that there were many spectators who thought that Balmerino would have also got closer to Alleged than the 1½ lengths if Ron Hutchinson had made his move earlier. Piggott appeared to catch them all on the blind side. Vintage stuff from the Long Fella.

Dunfermline returned to Longchamp for the Prix Royal-Oak later in October. With Gregarious broken down, Sea Boat was purchased to be the pacemaker.

Says Lord Porchester: 'Dunfermline had a terrible journey over to France. She was held up at every turn. There were air traffic control problems and also fog. It was a mistake to run her anyway. She was over the top and had her winter coat.

'Even so she ran on well to be third behind Rex Magna.' On Doncaster form she would have beaten the first two in a hack canter.

Ironically Dunfermline never won again after her triumph over Alleged. She ran three times as a four-year-old, but never recovered the form which caused an ecstatic Yorkshire crowd to will her over the line ahead of Alleged.

Says Lord Porchester of The Queen's jockey: 'He reminds me so very much of Gordon Richards. Both of them never admit defeat. They go on riding from any position.'

Carson's win on Rhyme Royal at Newbury on 20 October 1977 will remain in my memory as Carson at his brilliant best. The Queen's two-year-old was making his debut, and at half-way Carson seemed to have no chance. Then the driving power of the little Scot seemed to be translated to Rhyme Royal and, increasing his stride, he battled on to get up on the line by a short head from Pat Eddery on Persepolis. It was sheer brilliance.

'Yes, that was a marvellous win,' agrees Lord Porchester, 'but for me his best-ever display came in my colours on the filly Silk Stocking in York's Strensall Stakes on 5 September 1973.

'He must have been a furlong behind the leader at one time, or so it seemed. Then suddenly Carson began to work in his inspired style. From half way he kept on driving and got up to win by a head. He came back grinning and said: "Bloody miracle. An incredible animal!" In truth it was his incredible riding. I remember that I had come all the way back from Wales, where I had been on holiday. Quite frankly, I had given up all hope of winning until Willie started his run. It was unbelievable.'

Both The Queen and Lord Porchester are avid Carson fans. Reveals Lord Porchester: 'Harry Wragg was and Lester Piggott still is the outstanding waiting jockey. But Gordon and Willie are the driving type. I first noticed Willie when Jack Clayton engaged him to ride a winner for me at Folkestone. Jack said: "He's a good boy with Sam Armstrong."

'Willie is always his usual self in The Queen's company. He's always very polite. Far from tongue-tied. Just the opposite.

'One day at the races I was emphasizing a point to him and prodding him with my stick. I kept hitting him to make sure he understood.

'He had his own back. I injured an achilles tendon playing tennis at Milford and had to go to the races with my leg encased in plaster.'

Lord Porchester does a fine impression of the Carson squeaking laughter which Mike Yarwood would be proud of as he says: 'He came up and gave me a really hefty thump on the plaster with his whip. He really loved that.'

The man who has put so much into public life reveals that being racing manager to The Queen can have its difficult moments. He recalls: 'I backed Pinza at 33–1 for the Derby and watched the race in the Royal box. Of course, I had to contain myself as Her Majesty's Aureole was second. Actually I didn't have to worry. The Queen was just as happy, as we all wanted Gordon to win the Derby.

'You know Gordon won the Bessborough Stakes at Royal Ascot for me just after the war on Esquimalt. Raceform wrote, "There is only one Gordon Richards and he, and he alone, would have won on this horse."

'I presented Gordon with some gold cufflinks with the words inscribed on them. Willie Carson is the same. He wins on horses which nobody else would have won on.'

With that, Lord Porchester dashed off to check that Troy had settled in well at his new home. 'Yes, I'm a self-confessed enthusiast. So is Willie. He's the perfect gentleman. I hope he is the Royal jockey for many, many, many years to come,' he said. What a fine Royal accolade for Willie Carson.

13 'He simply never gives up'

Seven jockeys came laughing and joking out of the weighing-room at Newmarket's charming July course in 1977 for the Montrose Handicap . . . but there were only six runners!

Yes, you've guessed. Such was Willie Carson's total and complete absorption in day-to-day race-riding that he wandered out to the paddock for a race in which he didn't even have a ride.

The never-say-die Scot waited in the paddock for a full four minutes before he realized his error and left the paddock to loud applause. There is no doubt that Willie is greatly admired by the public. They have a warm affection for this game little trier.

'I was given a royal reception on the way back,' said Carson. 'I tried to get back without being spotted. I just mixed up the time of the race. I'm riding eight or nine horses every day. You weigh out, ride in the race, change colours and saddles. There's not much time to relax since I'm not exactly missing rides. I'm probably doing a bit too much.'

In reality Carson has been doing too much for years. Way back in 1972 he rode in 829 races to score 132 wins. Just look at the number of races (and winners) he has had since then. It's a fantastic record of dedication to one's job. In 1973 it was 883 rides (163 wins), 1974 – 908 (129), 1975 – 849 (131), 1976 – 865 (138), 1977 – 880 (160), 1978 – 986 (182), 1979 – 820 (142). This makes 7028 rides and 1177 winners in eight years. Usually statistics in sport are misleading, but not in Carson's case. They prove just how hard-working and consistent he has been.

In 1977 Carson conceded: 'I only feel tired talking about all the riding. But I do sometimes wonder why I bother to chase so hard when some of the others sit back and enjoy themselves. I suppose it's the way Sam Armstrong taught me.

'I don't want to go to an evening meeting for just one ride. But if it's got a chance I'm in the car and away.'

In 1978 there was even speculation that the flying Scot would become the first man since Sir Gordon Richards to ride 200 winners in a season. For years Willie has without doubt been the busiest jockey in Europe. Sir Gordon achieved the double century on twelve occasions in his fabulous career. In 1947 he set the all-time British record when he rode 269 winners – an achievement unlikely to be ever bettered. In 1933 Sir Gordon booted home 259 winners.

In 1978 when Willie neared the magic figure of 200, Sir Gordon told me: 'If any of the contemporary jockeys can ride 200 winners in one season then Willie is the man. His energy and enthusiasm are remarkable and he simply never knows when he is beaten.'

Major Hern, who quickly struck up a good working relationship with Carson, was soon giving this glowing testimony: 'I continually see Willie win races from positions where there was every justification for him to drop his hands – he simply never gives up.'

People who thought that Willie would top the double century in 1978 should remember his statement half way through the season. He said: 'It's a hell of a task. I have to find ninety-nine winners in fifteen weeks. That's how difficult it is.'

In 1977 Carson chalked up the seventh century of his career when winning on Petlady at Kempton Park on 31 August. A year later he was the fastest man to pass 100 since Lester Piggott in 1961. He went on to regain his title from Pat Eddery.

The previous year the last flickering hopes of taking the title from Eddery were extinguished by a seven-day ban imposed by the Newmarket stewards after he had finished second on Petty Purse behind Sookera in the William Hill Cheveley Park Stakes. The stewards also took the £11,412 second prize money from Petty Purse and placed the filly last.

At this stage of the season Carson trailed Pat Eddery by

fourteen winners, and when he returned to the saddle there was only seventeen days of the season left. Willie also lost his appeal against the suspension – and with it his last chance of the title.

Significantly the stewards returned Carson's deposit. After a two-hour hearing the stewards announced the final blow to Willie's challenge for the title.

Ironically, while Carson was losing his appeal in London, Eddery was bang in form at Brighton and rode a double. I saw the film of the Cheveley and considered that Carson's trouble was caused by Smarten Up moving over. There was some justification for Willie saying: 'A gap was there. It was not my fault that it closed.'

Carson still rode a 172-1 treble on the day of the Cheveley Park. Not even the prospect of a seven-day ban at this vital stage of the season could dim Carson's appetite for winners.

Although Carson was not champion in 1977 he was voted Jockey of the Year by the Horse Race Writers' Association. His Royal victories on Dunfermline in the Oaks and St Leger meant that he outpointed Lester Piggott, who had won the Arc on Alleged. Carson was the first jockey to win the Writers' award for the second time. Previous winners had not been eligible before but the rules were changed.

Cracked ribs dented hopes of winning the title, and the seven-day ban would have crushed most jockeys' enthusiasm. But not Carson. Had he become a bantamweight boxer I suspect that any fights he did lose would definitely have been on points. I can't see him being on the floor for long.

Boldboy had become one of Willie's favourites. He proved one of the toughest and most consistent horses in training and set a record for the amount of prize money won by a gelding. In the autumn of 1977 he finished his campaign when Willie drove him home by three-quarters of a length in the Challenge Stakes at Newmarket.

But in the Dewhurst Stakes Willie on Sexton Blake had to give second-best to Try My Best. And in the Champion Stakes he was again second, this time on Relkino behind Flying Water. Willie had finished second on Belfalas in the gruelling Newmarket marathon of the Cesarewitch. Now the same duo were to finish fourth behind Assured, although backed down to 9–2 favourite.

In 1978 Willie regained the title from Pat Eddery. They were neck and neck for much of the season, but in the end Willie surged ahead and won by an impressive 182–148 margin. After four years as the champion Pat Eddery had to hand the championship back to Carson. It must be said that Eddery's task was made much harder by the fact that Peter Walwyn's previous all-conquering Lambourn yard was devastated by the dreaded virus and Peter 'Mr Winners' Walwyn had a bad summer. From 110 winners in 1977 his haul slumped back to seventy.

It was perhaps inevitable that one day Walwyn would suffer. Dick Hern had three seasons when a cloud hung over the West Ilsley string. Now it was Walwyn's turn to see his magnificent stable grind to almost a halt. With typical honesty Walwyn said at one stage: 'I'm closing down and won't have runners for a week or two. I'm not running my horses for the sake of the bookies.' Ryan Price, a previous virus sufferer, recalls: 'When I got it Peter joked to me that I was just making excuses because my horses didn't go as fast as his. He soon found out the seriousness of the ruddy virus.'

Willie's champion year of 1978 soon clicked into top gear when he won the Rosebery Handicap at Kempton on Celtic Pleasure – his first ride of the season. Some 985 rides later he was back in the winner's enclosure on Harry Wragg's Court Barns at Doncaster – in his final ride of the campaign. Sheer honest graft in between gave the likeable pilot the championship he richly deserved.

This was the year of Try My Best, Robert Sangster's very inaptly named colt. He came to Newmarket for the 2000 Guineas with a reputation fit to blast any bookies' satchel wide open. He was backed down to evens favourite with a mountain of ante-post cash pouring on the Sangster, O'Brien, Piggott bandwagon. But Try My Best didn't only fail to win the Guineas . . . he was the first horse beaten and finished tailed off last. He was the layers' horse of the century.

Carson finished seventh on Admiral's Launch, who had run well to win the Ladbrokes Craven Stakes. Willie had his tenth ride in the Derby on Dick Hollingworth's Brigadier Gerard colt. This was a Derby when public support for Lester Piggott saw him start 4–1 favourite on the almost unknown O'Brien colt, Inkerman. Carson was to finish twelfth on Admiral's Launch. It was Dick Hern's fourteenth attempt to win the world's top Flat race. For Hern and Carson, their dream win was just twelve months away.

In the Oaks of 1978 Carson was sixth on The Queen's Tartan Pimpernel. This was the year when Greville Starkey, the well-known Newmarket dog impersonator and fancy shirt fancier, was reported to the Monopolies Commission for his Classic exploits. He won the English and Irish Derbys on Shirley Heights and the two Oaks on Fair Salinia. Little wonder he joked at the end of the season: 'I've paid so much income tax I now own the M1.'

By May it was clear that Carson and Eddery were going to be locked in a hectic battle for the top honour. Willie had the advantage of Eddery's being sidelined for four days in June by a red card from the French authorities. Carson powered home a Brighton treble at 55–1 on 27 June and drew level with Pat on sixty-five winners.

By July Carson had gone twenty-one winners ahead of Eddery, and his Herculean efforts in the saddle were fast becoming a daily entertainment for racegoers. Every time Carson climbed into the saddle you knew that you were on a trier.

On 5 July Carson rode five winners. He then dashed from one meeting to another all over the country and a cascade of winners poured through the powerhouse hands of the Scot.

One could only gasp at some of Carson's rides. His perpetual motion was translated to his rides. Horses which had no right to win were being urged home by the champion elect.

There's hardly a minute when he does not indulge in cheeky asides from his machine-gun patter. But once he is given the leg up, it's concentration all the way on the serious business of urging his mount home first. His black Ferrari roared 2000 miles a week sometimes to transport this remarkable man to yet another venue where he could score more winners.

At glorious Goodwood Willie was top jockey with six winners from the five-day meeting. He ended the rather special Sussex meeting with a four-timer on Eyelet, Town and Country, Cistus and Pilley Green. On 24 August Carson completed the fastest 100 since the days of Sir Gordon Richards when Going For Gold won the Corsham Handicap at Bath. Ironically Pat Eddery, now under great pressure to keep his title, was runner-up on La Pampa. The pair came very close to each other two furlongs out but the stewards, with no camera patrol film to help them, allowed the result to stand. It just wasn't Pat's year.

Later in the season we saw a typical piece of Carson genius in the saddle at Goodwood. Riding actor Albert Finney's useful filly, Quina, Carson pounced on a rather unsuspecting John Reid on the 6–5 favourite, Fancy Work, and short-headed him. It was one of countless displays from Willie where he turned defeat into victory by simply refusing to give in. He was a real whirlwind in that race.

Willie completed a double on Falls of Lora that October day. Pleased as he was by his double, the result which pleased him most of all was in fact at Nottingham. 'My first,' said a grinning Willie as he announced that Willie Sing's victory at Nottingham was his first as a successful breeder. His mare, Hay-Hay, had previously bred six seconds before Willie Sing had opened Carson's breeding record at Nottingham. Ironically it was Kipper Lynch, another ex-Sam Armstrong lad, who rode Willie Sing. Carson had one second on the two-year-old from three attempts.

Carson was well supported to win the season's last big Flat race, the William Hill November Handicap, at Doncaster on the John Dunlop-trained Falls of Lora. But the 7–1 second favourite finished fourth. The hustling Scot did win the very last race of the 1978 Flat season on Court Barns. With 182 winners Carson was champion again. He would have won by an even bigger margin but for one unlucky day at Ascot in September, when he was disqualified on two mounts.

Firstly Stanley Powell's The Adrianstan was disqualified after finishing first in the Swinley Forest Stakes, and then Town and Country was disqualified after dead-heating for second place. In both cases Willie's mounts had hung violently to the right in the closing stages.

But it was swings and roundabouts, as earlier in the season at Nottingham when Willie rode a 66–1 treble he was only awarded one race on Roja Roly after he had successfully objected to the first two past the line. Such was Willie's determination at the end of the season that he actually rode trebles on each of the last two days of the Flat.

In October Carson had another pleasing experience . . . he tamed the National Hunt jockeys at their own game. He was the only Flat jockey to take part in the Schroder Life Jockeys' Championship and proved a tremendous hit at the Horse of the Year Show. Hot foot from riding a winner at Goodwood, Carson arrived at Wembley to get up on Everest Jet Lag. Among the jump jockeys he beat were Bob Davies, Jeff King and Ian Watkinson. And all this was within twenty-four hours of riding a Goodwood double.

Willie's clear round in 34.35 seconds was half a second better than that year's Grand National winning rider, Bob Davies. Willie, in fact, very nearly missed out at Wembley. Officials failed to recognize him and for half an hour he was left outside the collecting ring.

Thrilled with his success Willie said happily: 'I go hunting in Leicestershire during the winter months so jumping isn't exactly new to me.'

Later Carson revealed: 'One of my regrets is that I never rode over hurdles – not fences. I would have loved to have won a race like the Schweppes. Now I know that it will never be done by me. I'm growing too old to think about that game. The chance has gone.'

Many a shrewd trainer has secured Willie's wonderful services for a handicap. Willie will never have an easier victory than when Ryan Price snapped him up to ride Sir Montagu in the 1976 Tote-Ebor. In what must have been the handicap snip of the century, Sir Montagu won by 8 lengths going away.

There is something about York which seems to bring the best out of Carson. Lord Porchester insists that his win there on Silk Stocking was the best he has seen.

The 1979 season saw a remarkable sporting achievement when Joe Mercer – 'forty-four years young' – became champion jockey for the first time. It was a very popular event, although Willie Carson had to be content with the runner-up position.

I'm sure the irony of the situation was not lost on veteran Joe, who had been replaced by Carson as first jockey to Dick Hern. Towards the end of his championship-winning year I quizzed Mercer about the end of his association at West Ilsley, a subject on which he had always maintained a dignified silence. Looking back, Joe told me: 'At the time it was a very unpleasant thing. Very bad. But I accept that the owners of the stable were going for somebody who would be around for a long time, and Willie was available.'

Joe is a lovely rider. Perfect style. He modelled himself on his late brother Manny and says: 'He is always in my mind. I was right behind him going down to the start at Ascot when he was killed. I think a lot about him and it seems only yesterday that we were riding together. I pass his grave at Newmarket every time I go to Henry Cecil's stables.'

The year of 1979 belonged to Willie Carson for his exploits on Troy and Joe Mercer for his championship win. But I have a feeling that Joe, still without a Derby win, would rather have won the Derby on Troy than gain the glory of being champion jockey. It's an interesting thought. And but for the action of Sir Michael Sobell and Sir Arnold Weinstock, who knows, it could have been Joe powering his way up the Epsom straight on Troy.

An incident in Stockholm towards the end of the 1979 season typified Willie's fierce dedication and courage. He was in Stockholm in front of an all-time record crowd of 10,000 to ride in the All-Star Jockeys' International. After finishing unplaced on Sirocco the horse decided in the unsaddling enclosure to put his full weight of 1000 pounds on Willie's right toe. After receiving painkillers, Willie said: 'I'll be all right tomorrow.' It was something of a scare, as the Stockholm incident was just one week before Willie was due to ride Troy in the Arc de Triomphe. But Carson's enthusiasm has proved many a doctor wrong, and sure enough the very next day he was back in the saddle at Newbury.

Carson has always been a man in a hurry. I'll never forget

the incident at Sandown in May 1978 when Willie dashed into the course but forgot to put the handbrake on his Ferrari. The car ran down the slope and crumpled into the back of trainer Michael Jarvis's brand-new Mercedes. Michael didn't quite see the funny side of it . . . he had only bought the car a week before.

Willie's keenness to go fast has thrilled racegoers . . . but not the police. In December 1978 he pulled off a treble of motoring summonses in twelve days.

At Newbury he was first fined £105 after pleading guilty to speeding. Magistrates heard that he was driving his £14,000 Ferrari sports car at 85 m.p.h. in a 60 m.p.h. limit area near Newbury. It was stated that he overtook fifteen lorries 'in seconds'.

Four days later at Newport Pagnell Willie was fined £100 after it was found that he had driven at 106 m.p.h. on the M1. The magistrates said it was only because of his job and the isolated area in which he lived that he would not be disqualified.

At York Carson completed the unwanted treble. It was stated that he left a traffic warden in a flat spin on his way to York races. As he pointed his sports car through a gap in the traffic at a busy junction he hit 15½ stone traffic warden Bob Davison, who was on point duty.

The warden was bowled over and left on his back as Carson and his girl friend roared off. Said Davison: 'All I saw was a face peering through the steering wheel. I thought that a child was driving it.'

Willie was fined £150, but because of a technicality in the totting-up procedure he was not disqualified from driving. He was found guilty of careless driving and failing to stop for a warden.

As he left the court Carson said: 'They say that bad luck always comes in threes. After twenty years' clean driving I've had a basinful this month.

'And on top of that I never rode a winner at York that day.'

Punters have few cases of summonsing Carson for slowness.

14 Terrific Troy

'You know, I don't think that I would have won the Derby on Troy. I wouldn't have had the tremendous patience of Willie Carson. He had the courage to wait until the horse did it all for him.'

Nothing strange in that you may think. . . . I know hundreds who wouldn't have won on Troy . . . but I was listening to arguably the greatest jockey of all-time, Sir Gordon Richards.

The fabulous idol of the first half of the twentieth century rode 4870 winners and was champion jockey twenty-six times.

'When Troy was right at the back of the field in the Derby on the incline up to the top of the hill at Epsom, I would have been very tempted to give him a backhander and that might have wrecked his chance,' reasons racing's shortest knight.

Autumn rain lashed against the study window of his Berkshire home as Sir Gordon recalled the highlights of his career and how he became racing manager to Willie Carson's two main owning parties, Sir Michael Sobell and Sir Arnold Weinstock, and Lady Beaverbrook.

I commented that Carson's style is often likened to that of Sir Gordon himself. The man with the twinkle in his sharp, brown eyes replied: 'No, I wouldn't say that.

'I think Willie Carson has a style of his very own. He never gives up and because of this, you never know that a Carson-ridden horse is beaten until the race is over.

'He has already been champion and I think he's going to be around for a long, long time.

'Willie gave Troy an excellent ride in the Derby. In the early stages of the Derby I was always very conscious of my position.

I was usually on a fancied runner and it was always in my mind that the owner, trainer and all the masses in the crowd would be looking for me and wondering why I was so far back.

'As I say, with Troy I would have been tempted to give him a backhander early on. That would have been a big mistake. No, Willie showed tremendous courage that day. Brilliant. He simply had the sense to leave him alone.'

Sir Gordon gazed out at the wintry weather and warmed his hands by the fire. Apart from his short, stocky frame that's the first thing you notice about Sir Gordon – his gentle, sympathetic hands which controlled horses in 21,843 races.

Millions idolized Sir Gordon, nicknamed Moppy because of his thick black hair. When they invested sixpenny doubles and trebles they always knew that they were on a trier. A similar modern-day betting-shop principle applies to Willie Carson.

Sir Gordon had a reputation as straight as a Roman road. His integrity in a sport graced by lords and louts alike has always been unquestionable.

Little wonder that when the BBC decided to screen four sporting programmes called *Maestro* in the autumn of 1979, Sir Gordon was the first subject, followed by Tom Finney, Fred Perry and Henry Cotton.

I attended a special press screening of the programme when Sir Gordon was present. Later at his home he chuckled: 'They filmed most of it here.

'I was a bit worried about it. I'm no Clark Gable but I was pleased with the outcome.'

The programme on Sir Gordon by Julian Wilson ably spotlighted the great man's career and his gentle, kindly personality.

One of twelve children – four died young – of a Shropshire miner, Sir Gordon became the most respected man of the Turf. It is interesting that when Willie Carson won the 200th Derby on Troy he immediately said that he had one regret . . . illness prevented Sir Gordon from being present to see the triumph.

But 'Moppy' has personal memories of most of the big racing moments of this century. Like the occasion when he was a stable lad at Jimmy White's private stables at Foxhill, Wiltshire.

Playing soccer for the stable team, his side were awarded a penalty. Recalls Sir Gordon: 'I always played right-back but I wanted the left-back to take the penalty. The score was 3–3 with minutes to go.

'Mr White shouted out that if I took the penalty and scored I would be given my first ride in a proper race. I tucked the ball into the net and was duly given my first leg-up in public on Clockwork at Lingfield towards the end of 1920. We finished fourth in a nursery.

'Perhaps my funniest moment came at Leicester when a certain Captain Vivian was acting as starter for the very first time.

'At one time everybody in racing thought I was well in with all the starters, judges, the lot. This chap kept looking down at us at the start and shouting, "Are you ready, Gordon?" I was facing round the wrong way, but when he yelled out again: "Are you ready, Gordon?" Harry Wragg shouted back, "Yes, sir," and off they went.

'The rest of the field were down in the dip when I eventually got my horse round the right way and got off. Harry Wragg was always nick-named the Head Waiter but he didn't wait that day. He fooled the starter before we even got going.'

Sir Gordon became the Sir Jack Hobbs of racing, idolized wherever he went. Throughout his career he was not involved in the slightest hint of a scandal. Like Hobbs, he was the Master.

In 1933 he made racing history by riding 259 winners, beating Fred Archer's previous record of 246 winners set up in 1885. In the same year he created yet another record when he rode eleven successive winners.

Sir Gordon's friendly smile comes flashing back as he recounts: 'At Chepstow I rode six winners on the first day and the first five on the second day.

'Of course, it was unbelievable. When I got to seven or eight I couldn't credit it. But it kept going and by the twelfth race the entire weighing-room were going mad.

'Actually I finally finished third, beaten a neck and a head, on Eagle Ray. Out of the twelve rides he was considered the biggest certainty of the lot – couldn't possibly be beaten. I remember that it was a young Doug Smith as an apprentice who ended the consecutive wins.'

Sir Gordon had twenty-eight attempts before he won the Derby on Pinza in 1953, the same year that he was knighted by the newly crowned Queen.

More happy memories come flooding back for Sir Gordon. Unlike Willie Carson who struck Epsom Derby gold at the eleventh attempt, Sir Gordon had years of Derby disappointments. His win on Pinza was the twenty-eighth and final try.

'I rode in my first Derby in 1924 on Skyflight and finished nineteenth. Years went by, and my luck never seemed to change. I was second to Charlie Smirke and Windsor Lad on Easton in 1934. And second to Charlie again on Taj Ajbar in 1936 when he won on Mahmoud.

'Then I was third in 1938, second in 1939, and then third in 1942. Several times I picked the wrong horse and had to struggle in down the field when horses I had passed over won the race.

'I always seemed to turn down the winners. On six or seven mounts I was beaten before we ever got to the starting gate. The Derby is not only about class horses, it's all about temperament. That's where Troy was so good. The parade never bothered him at all.

'Often I had horses down at the start who were so badly affected by the huge crowd and the parade that they were like jellyfish.

'In 1953 I was sure that it was going to be my last season. But I still didn't have that Derby win to my credit. It was something very vital missing. Had I retired and not won the Derby I think I would have woken up every day for the rest of my life and straight away had a little curse to myself.

'Pinza was like Troy. A horse you grew to love. He was more massive than Troy. He was so strong that he could have pulled the Cornish Riviera behind and still won.

'Oh yes, Pinza was a great horse. It was just such a big disappointment that he was such a failure at stud.'

Sir Gordon's seemingly best chance of Derby success had come in 1947 when he rode Tudor Minstrel. The previous year he had won four races on the two-year-old, and then they made hacks of their rivals in the 2000 Guineas a year later. After his 8 lengths' win at Newmarket Sir Gordon seemed certain to end the Derby hoodoo.

Starting at 7–4 on, Tudor Minstrel became the bookies' pet horse of the century when he was a well-beaten fourth behind Pearl Diver. It was a bleak, rainy day at Epsom, and Pearl Diver's colours were similar to those of Tudor Minstrel.

As Pearl Diver darted for home out of the mist the huge crowd went mad. 'Go on, Gordon,' they roared excitedly, thinking that at last he had wrecked the Derby jinx. Then a great hush fell over the rain-lashed Surrey Downs when the crowd realized that Gordon was struggling back in fourth place.

Recalls Sir Gordon: 'That day I was very much aware that I simply had to have Tudor Minstrel always well up with the leaders. But he was fighting me most of the way and I was fighting him. He led with his right foot and that's curtains at Epsom. You must have a horse which leads with his left foot to have any chance of going smoothly down Tattenham Corner.'

Sir Gordon did not set the record books alight when he switched to training. Yet strangely he says: 'I don't miss the riding at all. But I do so miss the training. After all those thirty-four years of riding I was bound to get a little tired of it. But training, that's different.

'There's a tremendous amount of satisfaction in getting a horse to concert pitch, developing him, muscling him up . . . and then seeing him win a race. I used to love it.'

After training for Sir Michael Sobell and Sir Arnold Weinstock he became their racing manager. He says: 'London Cry did start it all. We were lucky. Perhaps if things had been different, those owners would not have been so keen to stay in the game.

'At first we used to go to the sales, but I learned after a while that it was silly to pay big prices. The best way – and probably the only way – to succeed in racing is to breed your own horses.

'When you have your own stud and mares you know just how the colts and fillies have been educated. When you go to the sales, you know the breeding but you don't really know how the horses have been nursed along.

'As I say with Troy, temperament is so vital in a Classic

horse. You have got to know how the horses have been looked after in early life.'

Sir Arnold Weinstock praises his son Simon for the breeding knowledge which resulted in Troy being born at the Ballymacoll Stud in County Meath, Eire.

He told me: 'The year before Troy was born we had not used Petingo as a stallion. Simon said that it was a big mistake. If I had had my way Troy would never have been born.

'Petingo cost about 6000 guineas, which was quite expensive at that time, but Simon urged us to send him to our mare, La Milo, who was by Hornbeam. La Milo won four times and was, ironically, by Pinza.

'When the foals are born, my father-in-law and I gather in a few names which we think will be suitable. Usually we try and think of something which is associated with the mother or father.

'But in Troy's case he got his name because my son was a classical scholar and we thought it suitable. I like short names.'

Recalls Sir Gordon: 'I first saw Troy as a foal at Sir Michael Sobell's stud in Ireland. Even as a foal he certainly caught the eye. In the paddocks he didn't fiddle about. He always moved nicely at that age which is a very good sign.'

Troy's life then switched to Major Dick Hern's stables at West Ilsley. This outstanding horseman had gone to the Berkshire stables in 1963.

Previously he had been at Newmarket as trainer to the late Major Holliday. The first day that Dick rode out at Newmarket he passed genial trainer Ryan Jarvis, who quipped: 'Good morning, Dick. I suppose you brought your toothbrush. It's all you will need.'

But Hern stayed from 1957 to 1963 and was successful. But like Sir Gordon Richards, Derby victory escaped this likeable handler.

In 1962 he suffered the agony of seeing Hethersett being brought down at Tattenham Hill when he had a great chance. Later he confirmed this by winning the St Leger.

By 1969 Dick Hern had run fourteen horses in the Derby. Hethersett was clearly an unlucky loser, and so too was Remand, who was fourth in 1968. Recalls Joe Mercer: 'Even

Lester who won on Sir Ivor thought that he was the one. He'd won the Royal Lodge on him as a two-year-old.

'But from Chester onwards the Major's horses started to cough one by one. Sooner or later it had to be Remand. Sure enough when I went out to the paddock for the Derby I didn't even recognize Remand. He was in a bad state and was far from his best.'

Proud Chieftain (fifth), Remand (fourth), Bustino (fourth), Smuggler (eighth), Relkino (second) had been Dick Hern's prominent Derby runners. There had been disappointments besides the luckless Hethersett.

But Dick Hern's Derby agony was about to end.

As a two-year-old Troy ran four times, winning twice and being placed twice.

Recalls Sir Arnold Weinstock: 'Because of business I never saw Troy as a two-year-old actually on a racecourse. I did, however, pop down to the stables and see Willie ride him in gallops on Saturday mornings.

'As a two-year-old I did see him as 'a Derby candidate. But Dick's methods of training the youngsters means that he never drives them to fitness. He brings them along gently. He always does no more than what the horses show him they are capable of.'

Sir Gordon Richards told me: 'Troy kept developing all the time and with a horse like that you never knew where he would stop. He was far from disgraced when he was second in the Royal Lodge. Willie had a battle to beat Lyphard's Wish and then having done that, Ela-Mana-Mou came and pipped both of them. Willie always insisted that if the race had been run again he would reverse the placings.

'Ela-Mana-Mou was a good colt so we knew that Troy had done well. In a previous race he had actually beaten Ela-Mana-Mou.'

Looking back to the start of Troy's three-year-old career, Sir Arnold Weinstock says: 'In the spring I was hopeful that Troy would be a Derby horse. I'd backed him for the race the previous autumn after the Royal Lodge. But one is never advised to take a strong view of Dick Hern's three-year-olds early on in the season. He never asks them a big question at home.'

'There is no betting in the stable, and there is no incentive for the horses to be worked flat out on the gallops. They are tried at full tilt only on the racecourses.'

Troy made his three-year-old debut in the Classic Trial Stakes at Sandown on 28 April. Willie Carson had to use all his strength to get Troy, the 7–4 on favourite, up to catch Two of Diamonds by a neck in the last few strides. But Sir Gordon was happy. He recalled: 'He had to race by himself and I thought, "Poor old Troy. All on his own and in heavy going." It was only a neck but I was pleased.'

When I spoke to Carson at the start of the season, he was his usual happy self. On his hopes of regaining the jockeys' title he would not be drawn. Confident but not prepared to make any Ali-like predictions, I thought. Actually he did say, 'More Light is certain to be my ride in the 200th Derby.' It's funny how a few months can completely switch the course of events.

By early May Troy and The Queen's Milford emerged as his Derby candidates. But at Chester on 10 May he received a setback in the final contest on Harry Wragg's Lidgate. Attempting to make all, he was close to home when Lidgate went crashing and Carson was dashed to hospital with a broken right collarbone.

Typically, he discharged himself the very next morning and was back as a viewer at Chester, although still obviously suffering from the effects of torn knee ligaments.

Pat Eddery stepped in for the ride on More Light in the Mecca Dante at York, where the colt virtually ruled out his Derby chances when he started favourite but finished fourth.

Carson had won on Milford in Ascot's White Rose Stakes and he was a live Derby hope. He was by Mill Reef and Highclere's first foal. Reports indicated that he was catching pigeons at West Ilsley on the gallops but was something of a lively young gentleman.

With Willie still sidelined, Joe Mercer went down memory lane and donned the Royal silks to ride Milford in the Ladbrokes Lingfield Derby Trial on 12 May. Starting at 11–4 on, Milford coasted home by 7 lengths. Oddly enough he seemed to be well suited to Lingfield's gradients and turns, but it was to be a different story at Epsom.

For once the great Lester Piggott Derby-ride guessing game was not the trailer to the world's greatest race. All the pre-race speculation for the 200th Derby now centred on whether Carson would pick Troy or The Queen's Milford.

Later Carson was to confess: 'There was never any real doubt. I wanted to ride Troy and really fancied him.' But turning down The Queen's Derby colt in a particularly interesting year was to prove a headache.

In the Predominate Stakes at Goodwood on 23 May, Troy made hacks of rivals and won by 7 lengths – the same winning margin as Milford at Lingfield.

Troy did a slow time at Goodwood but was very impressive. 'Tomorrow, gentlemen. I want the evening to consider it,' was Carson's quick comment when he dismounted from Troy. He had been out of action for two weeks with his broken collarbone but was straight back in the winner's enclosure.

Looking back, Sir Arnold Weinstock says: 'I was very anxious for Willie to make up his mind. I pressed Lord Porchester to try and make him decide. I urged, "Get him to choose," but he would not until after the Goodwood race, which was fair enough really. I was just anxious to line up reserves if he opted for Milford. We approached Lester Piggott, and even Yves Saint-Martin was mentioned.

'But Willie never let on.'

After Troy's win I wrote in the *Sun*: 'Willie Carson will this morning turn down the Royal prerogative to ride for The Queen in the 200th Derby.

'Not even the guarantee of a knighthood will make Carson desert Troy for 6 June at Epsom. I confidently expect the perky champion to reject Her Majesty's Milford.'

Sure enough the next day Carson emerged from the weighing-room at Goodwood to say: 'It's Troy.' Lester was then approached to ride Milford.

Before Carson made his decision, Dick Hern admitted. 'I'm very glad it's not me who is making the decision but Carson.

'I don't honestly know which one I would pick. Troy simply had a nice bit of work. It was a delightfully easy race, and I now have two real live Derby hopes.

'Troy has an ideal temperament and will not be affected in any way by all the hullabaloo at Epsom. He won't care less when the band strikes up. His trainer will be more nervous – that's for sure.

'Milford is a more excitable type, and this is always a slight worry. But he has never done anything actually wrong in a race.'

Even after Carson's decision, bookies feared the usual Piggott plunge, especially in the Royal colours, and Milford was 5–1 favourite. Troy was freely backable at 8–1.

At Goodwood Ryan Price had pressmen reeling with laughter when he was asked what tactics he would give Brian Taylor on Lake City in the Derby. Boomed Ryan: 'I've told him that just because he once pissed off in front on a million to one outsider and won, I'll shoot him if he does the same on Lake City.' Ryan was somewhat confused when, having instructed Lake City to be held up in the Guineas, Harry Demetriou's colt had led 4 furlongs out. Regarding front-running tactics, Ryan was referring to Snow Knight's 50–1 Derby win in the hands of Taylor in 1974. The Derby has become an obsession for Ryan and he freely admits: 'When I win it, they can bury me the next day. No man will ever die happier.'

All roads led to Epsom Downs on 6 June. Thousands of racegoers jammed the roads. Coaches galore inched their way to the course – a sharp contrast to the transport which must have been used way back in 1780 when Diomed won the first Derby at 6–4.

Sir Arnold Weinstock recalls: 'Troy worked on the Downs and went well. Willie came back, gave his usual grin and said, "Went all right." That was enough, I knew that he was happy.

'I have total confidence in Willie. We don't have to tell him anything about how to ride in a race. Willie is such a lovely little man that you don't have to tell him when he's ridden a bad race. But he didn't apologize for anything he did on Troy at Epsom.'

While thousands struggled through the traffic snarl-ups around Epsom at 11.30 a.m. Sir Arnold Weinstock was still in his G E C office, masterminding the vast business empire.

At 4.30 p.m. he was back at his desk in the heart of London

. . . and in between he and his father-in-law won the 200th Derby.

Reveals Sir Arnold: 'Our party flew to Epsom by helicopter from Battersea. That's how I was able to do some work in the morning and still return after the race back to the office.'

Sir Gordon Richards had suffered a trapped nerve. The great little man watched the race with his brother at his Kintbury home. His next door neighbour is Keith Piggott. It's fascinating how one little street contains arguably the two most famous names the Turf has ever known.

The day started badly for Carson. Riding for Denys Smith he finished stone-last on newcomer Ravaduos in the opening race.

Then on Miss Noname (of Doncaster fame) he was unplaced in the second race. Then came the race he will never forget.

Perhaps Troy's racing manager Sir Gordon Richards sums the triumph up best: 'Well, I began to lose interest. He was so far back I began to wonder whether he'd finish last not first.'

Sir Arnold agrees: 'At Tattenham Corner I started to realize that he was running stones below his form and I couldn't possibly see him getting into the frame.'

As expected, Joe Mercer made a very early move to the front on Lyphard's Wish. The early pace was a cracker and Troy simply couldn't keep up.

Carson was soon seen to be riding for his life, and Troy's hopes seemed doomed. At Tattenham Corner he was 'out with the washing' and had no apparent chance. He was boxed in and well to the rear of the field.

Sir Gordon insists: 'It was up to this point that Willie showed his tremendous courage. I'm certain that as he struggled to go the early pace I would have been tempted to give him a backhander and he would probably have cut his throat after one flick. You can burst 'em with one flick if you try to keep up early on in a race.'

Two furlongs from home Lyphard's Wish dropped back, and it seemed to be between Dickens Hill, Northern Baby and Ela-Mana-Mou. But Carson could be spotted, driving like a steam piston on Troy.

Then millions saw a sight they will never forget. Says Sir

Arnold, who was watching from the Jockey Club stand: 'I could see Willie trying to move to the outside and thought, "Well he must think there's something there. We could possibly be third."'

Sir Gordon says: 'After losing interest, I noticed that Troy had moved quietly up at Tattenham Corner. I thought with a bit of luck we might be third.

'But when Willie pulled him out and gave him a backhander it was like an electric shock. From having no chance he had shot to the front and was playing wih them. It was amazing.'

Troy had 7 lengths to spare over Dickens Hill. Lester Piggott and Milford had been prominent for a long way but finally finished tenth. Lester said: 'He hated the course and kept changing his legs.'

While the hacks were composing, 'Troy makes the others look like wooden horses,' Carson came back to a terrific reception. And he was just the man to steal the show at the television, radio and press interviews afterwards.

In the *Sun* the next day, under headlines of 'Troy's Magic' and 'Carson wrapped it up in four strides,' I wrote: 'Willie Carson and Troy ran away with the 200th Derby to destroy the theory that jockeys are racing's worst judges.

'The flying Scot two weeks ago picked Troy in preference to The Queen's Milford, who is also trained by Dick Hern.

'It was the kind of decision men were once sent to the Tower for. But Carson had the last laugh and Troy won by 7 lengths. It was the longest winning distance since Steve Donoghue booted home Manna by 8 lengths in 1925.

'For Carson it was a fairy-tale come true. At the ninth attempt he erased particularly the horror memory of two years ago. Then he appeared to have the race won on Hot Grove only for Lester Piggott to pounce on The Minstrel.

'Carson said: "I was in trouble in the early part of the race. I needed a pair of binoculars to see the leaders. Most of the field were in front of me turning into the straight and I had experienced terrible trouble getting past Laska Floko, who was going backwards.

'"But when Troy saw daylight he simply took off. I expected him to quicken but I honestly never realized that he had this blinding turn of speed.

'"He's the best colt I have ever ridden and will be unbeatable in the Irish Derby. The whole race ended in four strides."'

Wise-cracking Willie was whisked away to the Royal box. He said. 'The Queen was absolutely delighted. After our chat you would have thought that I had won the race for her on Milford.

'Let's face it, if you turn down a ride for The Queen it's got to be for a winner.'

Sir Arnold Weinstock says: 'Troy's time for the last furlong was exceptional. I was invited to the Royal box. It was something of a bitter-sweet occasion.'

Then the big-business tycoon was away by helicopter and back to his office. In the evening he celebrated with a small party for six at the Connaught Hotel.

Carson commented: 'The plan I had was to track Lyphard's Wish, but I just couldn't go the pace. Then I had trouble with Laska Floko. When I hit the front I thought of Lester two years ago. But he didn't come this time.'

Dick Hern immediately revealed that the owners were keen to run Troy in the Arc de Triomphe. He added, 'I was sure that he would quicken, and he had behaved so well in the parade.'

The next day's racing at Epsom was abandoned after a freak thunderstorm. Dick Hern climbed the thousand steps up to the press room at the top of the Epsom grandstand. He discussed Troy and plans to go for the Irish Derby. After years attempting to win the Blue Riband, the Major had triumphed. He sipped champagne with pressmen. He laughed loudly. I've seldom seen a man more modestly thrilled at his success than Dick Hern.

Carson had ended one statistic as well. Until Troy cantered over his rivals, Willie and Doug Smith were the only champion jockeys since way back to Billy Higgs in 1907 never to win the Derby. That had been put right in spectacular style. Joe Mercer teamed up with Doug Smith after he became champion in 1979.

Troy started at 9–4 on for the Irish Derby. He'd been 6–1 at Epsom. Incidentally at Epsom Dickens Hill and Northern Baby covered the last 2 furlongs in the same time as Shirley

Heights the previous year – yet Troy won by 7 lengths!

The 7 length win at Epsom over Dickens Hill was reduced to 4 lengths. But it was another easy victory and something of a muddling race. The Bart led 5 furlongs out and the field began to get strung out. In fact one commentator did pass the comment at half-way, 'Willie Carson and Troy have it all to do.' Didn't he remember Epsom?

Willie Carson again had to rustle Troy along in the early stages, but they came flying through to hit the front over a furlong out and stayed on well. Sir Arnold Weinstock recalls: 'Actually Willie did say that he thought at the Curragh that he had gone to the front a bit too soon.'

Next stop for Troy was the King George VI and Queen Elizabeth Diamond Stakes on 28 July, which is fast rivalling the Arc as the best all-age race in Europe. After the 7 and 4 length wins, this time it was just 1½ lengths to spare over Gay Mecene.

Carson left nothing to chance, but it was an efficient win rather than the spell-binding Derby victories. But the pace never suited Troy, and his winning time was the slowest since another dual Derby hero, Nijinsky, in 1970. He was almost 7 seconds slower than the record-holder Grundy in 1975. Troy's pacemaker, Road to Glory, never had the field at full tilt.

This took Troy's winnings to a European record of £364,000. The owners never considered the St Leger; the Arc was the big autumn aim, and at Ascot Sir Arnold Weinstock indicated that Kempton's New September Stakes would be his preliminary race before going to France.

Sir Arnold recalls: 'I never contemplated going for the Benson and Hedges Gold Cup at York. I was abroad at Salzburg listening to some Mozart at his birthplace. It was never in mind that Troy would race again so soon.

'Dick rang me up and said that Willie was very keen to go for the Benson. I told him, "You're crazy. He's just had a fairly hard race and it would not be sensible to go for a race so soon over 1¼ miles." Added to that, I was sure that people would think that we were being greedy.

'But Dick said that Willie insisted it would be a good idea to run him at York. I wasn't too happy but eventually agreed.'

Again Carson was soon at work in the early stages of the race and the wonder colt was all out after 2 furlongs. A quarter of a mile from home he quickened to take the lead. Willie seemed to drop his hands a little and Troy thought that he had done enough and it was a rapidly reducing three-quarters of a length as Crimson Beau pressed to be second.

Raceform noted: 'It's difficult to envisage defeat in the Arc.'

Sir Gordon was still not fully fit, but watched again on television. He reasoned: 'Troy was a truly great Derby winner, and at York when Willie let him down he thought he had done enough and put the brake on in a few strides.'

I remember the after-race excitement in the winner's enclosure at York. People pressed Sir Arnold for details of the forthcoming syndication. Dick Hern said, 'This is the best horse I have ever trained.' There was a general hustle and bustle. But the coolest customer in the enclosure was Troy himself.

Sir Arnold told me: 'Some horses you have a relationship with. Some you positively dislike. London Cry, Crucible, Reform and Troy have been my favourites.

'Troy looks down his nose at you and I'm sure he thinks we are inferior. He's a princely individual. He feels he is somebody. He's a very superior person. When he travelled on planes with other horses, he knew that they were mere hacks and growled and roared at them.

'Sadly his mother, La Milo, had a swelling on her leg and had to be put down three months after Troy's birth.'

I consider that Troy would have trotted up in the St Leger, he'd have won turning hand-springs. But having been syndicated for £7.5 million, Troy's farewell was in the Arc de Triomphe. The day was 7 October . . . a lengthy 161 days since he had made his first appearance as a three-year-old way back in April. It would have been the training feat of the century by Dick Hern to have rounded off Troy's terrific year by winning the Paris thriller.

Sir Gordon Richards is as superstitious as the next racing man. 'I always used to raise my hat to a chimney sweep on the way to the races,' he says.

'After I missed Troy in the Derby I was reluctant to go and

see him in action at the tracks again. I thought that if I didn't watch him on television I'd put a hoo-doo on him.

'Then, having stayed away all summer when he was unbeaten, I went and did it all. I went over to Longchamp. I never ought to have gone.'

In reality it was the toughness of a long, hard season which beat Troy into third place in the Arc. He finished 4 lengths behind the filly Three Troikas. Like Nijinsky he was to experience defeat as a three-year-old in the massive Longchamp straight. Nijinsky also lost in the Champion.

A huge Paris crowd came to salute a brilliant horse. And there were so many English racegoers present that the exclusive paddock bar looked like the dive bar at Newmarket on Guineas day.

Troy strolled into the tree-lined paddock as though he didn't have a worry in the world. He was extremely calm, and one could understand Sir Arnold's claim that he is a superior being as he glanced round at his rivals with an almost contemptuous stare.

As usual Willie was soon at work, bustling Troy along to keep up with the early pace. The rain-soaked ground did not assist Troy's challenge. But at the long sweeping turn into the straight, Carson had moved Troy into a challenging position.

As Carson delivered his challenge, Troy roared into top gear, but the acceleration we had gasped at previously was missing. The 4–5 favourite was snookered.

Willie said realistically: 'No excuses. But a fresh Troy would have murdered 'em. He's had a long, hard season.'

There is no doubt in my mind that if Troy had raced against Three Troikas at any other time of the season he would have won with ease.

Sir Arnold Weinstock took defeat well. But he did have that little feeling that the crowd had not seen the best of his horse. He said: 'There was a little give in the ground, and this was not the same Troy who won two Derbys. I'm tempted to keep him in training specially to come back here and win the Arc.'

That, of course, will not happen. Troy was soon off to stud. Mention must be made of his faithful stable lad, David Gillespie. He was just nineteen, and had only left his Blyth,

Northumberland, home three years before to join Dick Hern.

He bought £2 of extra strong mints every week for Troy . . . the colt who became worth a mint.

Of the Arc run Dick Hern said: 'He ran a super race, but he has such a magnificent action and the soft going meant that he never bounced off the top of the ground.'

Sir Gordon reasoned: 'He'd had a long season in the very top class. And never forget that horses are not machines.

'Troy and Willie were well suited . . . two great battlers. Troy had more quality than my favourite, Pinza.

'For years men will sit in a pub on a Sunday night and argue whether Troy was better than Nijinsky. Or was Mill Reef better than them all? That's the great thing about racing . . . and there's nothing like it.'

Some thought that Troy should have been kept in training as a four-year-old. Reasoned Sir Arnold Weinstock of his 1979 Racehorse of the Year: 'The racecourse is our laboratory. We test the value of the hypothesis of breeding.

'With Troy we proved the case. It's more important to breed his successors than to race as a four-year-old.'

Sir Arnold, who backed Troy at 50–1 for the Derby after the Royal Lodge, invited his staff at GEC headquarters for a champagne party to celebrate the colt's win. 'Just for an hour – then it was back to work,' he grins.

I agree with Sir Gordon . . . 'Troy was a truly great Derby winner.'

Horses he slammed in the Derby went on to win the Eclipse, the Champion, the English, Irish and French St Legers, Royal Ascot's King Edward Stakes and the Princess of Wales' stakes at Newmarket.

But just how good is Troy's partner . . . Willie Carson?

There is no man better qualified to judge than Raceform's most experienced race-reader, John 'Hawk-eye' Sharratt. Since 1946 his binoculars have focussed on all the top jockeys. He has expertly viewed over 40,000 races, and his comments in the note-book are invaluable for professional gamblers.

Sharratt, whose kindly personality and tidy appearance resembles more a respected village doctor, told me: 'Willie Carson is terribly strong for somebody of his weight. Come to think of it, I can't recall ever seeing a stronger man for his weight. If you want a horse who needs a good kicking, slapping and driving handling then Carson is your man.

'If you want the pushing kind of action, you couldn't find anybody better than Willie.

'You never see him giving up, and that's where he pinches a hell of a lot of races from the others. You never see him sitting up in the saddle. He never eases 'em up. Of course, sometimes he has his head down and is going hell for leather so strongly that he may get boxed in without realizing what has happened around him.

'Carson certainly has the same kind of determination as Sir Gordon Richards. I well remember that wonderful ride he gave The Queen's two-year-old, Rhyme Royal, at Newbury. He gave the colt a tremendous ride.

'In 1979 there were two terrific examples of Carson's brilliance at his style of riding at Brighton. On 5 July in the Withdean Claiming Stakes on Martinholme he absolutely outrode Pat Eddery on Can-Do-More from the foot of the hill and won by three-quarters of a length. I wrote in the note-book "under typical Carson driving", and that was it.

'It was sheer strength and determination. There's nobody more determined. Later that afternoon he was headed 3 furlongs on Coyote in the Littlehampton Stakes but refused to give in. I wrote that "riding like a pocket dynamo" he went on to win by six lengths.'

Over the years Sharratt has eyed Classics galore and plenty of lack-lustre sellers. He has seen the lot – from talented riders to cowboys and cossacks. His comments after some amateur riders' races match Ryan Price for colour.

I leave the last words to Sharratt about Willie Carson – a truly remarkable little man and brilliant jockey.

He says: 'If you could drop Willie Carson from a helicopter into a horse's saddle 2 furlongs from home he'd very – I stress very – seldom be beaten.'

Index

Names of horses are in *italic* type